THE
newbiology

ANIMAL CLONING

The Science of Nuclear Transfer

Joseph Panno, Ph.D.

☑®

Facts On File, Inc.

ɔɔɔ

For my wife, Diana,
who worked with me in the lab for many years,
and for my daughter Eleanor,
who knew about cells before she could read or write.

ɔɔɔ

ANIMAL CLONING: The Science of Nuclear Transfer

Copyright © 2005 by Joseph Panno, Ph.D.

Facts On File, Inc.
132 West 31st Street
New York NY 10001

Library of Congress Cataloging-in-Publication Data

Panno, Joseph.
   Animal cloning : the science of nuclear transfer / Joseph Panno.
      p. cm. — (New biology)
Includes bibliographical references and index.
   ISBN 0-8160-4947-5
   1. Cloning—Popular works. 2. Cell nuclei—Transplantation—Popular works.
I. Title.
   QH442.2.P26 2004
   660.6'5—dc22   2003025471

Text design by Erika K. Arroyo
Cover design by Kelly Parr
Illustrations by Richard Garratt and Joseph Panno

Printed in the United States of America

MP FOF 10 9 8 7 6 5 4 3 2 1

This book is printed on acid-free paper.

CONTENTS

ᗣᗧ

PREFACE

꘎

The New Biology set consists of the following six volumes: *The Cell, Animal Cloning, Stem Cell Research, Gene Therapy, Cancer,* and *Aging.* The set is intended primarily for middle and high school students, but it is also appropriate for first-year university students and the general public. In writing this set, I have tried to balance the need for a comprehensive presentation of the material, covering many complex fields, against the danger of burying—and thereby losing—young students under a mountain of detail. Thus the use of lengthy discussions and professional jargon has been kept to a minimum, and every attempt has been made to ensure that this be done without sacrificing the important elements of each topic. A large number of drawings are provided throughout the series to illustrate the subject matter.

The term *new biology* was coined in the 1970s with the introduction of recombinant DNA technology (or biotechnology). At that time, biology was largely a descriptive science in danger of going adrift. Microbiologists at the turn of the century had found cures for a few diseases, and biologists in the 1960s had cracked the genetic code, but there was still no way to study the function of a gene or the cell as a whole. Biotechnology changed all that, and scientists of the period referred to it as the new technique or the new biology. However, since that time it has become clear that the advent of biotechnology was only the first step toward a new biology, a biology that now includes nuclear transfer technology (animal cloning), gene therapy, and stem cell therapy. All these technologies are covered in the six volumes of this set.

The cell is at the very heart of the new biology and thus figures prominently in this book series. Biotechnology was specifically designed for studying cells, and using those techniques, scientists gained insights into cell structure and function that came with unprecedented detail. As knowledge of the cell grew, the second wave of technologies—animal cloning, stem cell therapy, and gene therapy—began to appear throughout the 1980s and 1990s. The technologies and therapies of the new biology are now being used to treat a wide variety of medical disorders, and someday they may be used to repair a damaged heart, a severed spinal cord, and perhaps even reverse the aging process. These procedures are also being used to enhance food crops and the physical characteristics of dairy cows and to create genetically modified sheep that produce important pharmaceuticals. The last application alone could save millions of lives every year.

While the technologies of the new biology have produced some wonderful results, some of the procedures are very controversial. The ability to clone an animal or genetically engineer a plant raises a host of ethical questions and environmental concerns. Is a cloned animal a freak that we are creating for our entertainment, or is there a valid medical reason for producing such animals? Should we clone ourselves, or use the technology to re-create a loved one? Is the use of human embryonic stem cells to save a patient dying from leukemia a form of high-tech cannibalism? These and many other questions are discussed throughout the series.

The New Biology set is laid out in a specific order, indicated previously, that reflects the natural progression of the discipline. That is, knowledge of the cell came first, followed by animal cloning, stem cell therapy, and gene therapy. These technologies were then used to expand our knowledge of, and develop therapies for, cancer and aging. Although it is recommended that *The Cell* be read first, this is not essential. Volumes 2 through 6 contain extensive background material, located in the final chapter, on the cell and other new biology topics. Consequently, the reader may read the set in the order he or she prefers.

ACKNOWLEDGMENTS

⫷⫸

I would first like to thank my friend and mentor, the late Dr. Karun Nair, for helping me understand some of the intricacies of the biological world and for encouraging me to seek that knowledge by looking beyond the narrow confines of any one discipline. The clarity and accuracy of the initial manuscript for this book was greatly improved by reviews and comments from Diana Dowsley and Michael Panno, and later by Frank Darmstadt, Executive Editor; Dorothy Cummings, Project Editor; and Anthony Sacramone, Copy Editor. I am also indebted to Ray Spangenburg, Kit Moser, Sharon O'Brien, and Diana Dowsley for their help in locating photographs for the New Biology set. Finally, I would like to thank my wife and daughter, to whom this book is dedicated, for the support and encouragement that all writers need and are eternally grateful for.

INTRODUCTION

Nature has been cloning animals, cells, and molecules for millions of years. Scientists got into the act just 34 years ago, when John Gurdon, a professor at Cambridge University in England, cloned a frog. Gurdon's experiment did not generate a great deal of interest at the time and was rarely discussed outside the world of research labs. In 1996, when Ian Wilmut, a researcher at the Roslin Institute in Scotland, cloned a sheep named Dolly, the reaction was dramatically different. The news of Dolly's birth was reported in every major newspaper and magazine around the world, and she quickly became the most celebrated (and certainly the most photographed) lamb in the history of animal husbandry. Wilmut was invited to speak before the Parliament of the United Kingdom and the Congress of the United States, after which the team leaders were interviewed to the point of exhaustion. Cloning a mammal sparked the public's imagination in a way that had not been seen since American astronauts got their white suits dirty on the surface of the moon. Cloning a sheep, unlike cloning a frog, brought the technology closer to home, making it both fascinating and frightening to a great many people.

The ability to clone a mammal was the culmination of research in cell and developmental biology that stretched back to the late 1800s. The idea of cloning an animal was originated by the German embryologist Hans Spemman in 1898 as a way of testing the developmental capacity of an adult cell nucleus and whether such a nucleus lost genes during the process of embryonic development. The techniques available in Spemman's time were not adequate to explore fully this question. Moreover, very little was known about the cell and, in particular, about the process of cell division. This information came only after the introduction of recombinant DNA technology in the 1970s. By the 1990s, enough had been learned about the cell and the properties of cell division to make mammalian cloning a possibility.

Although Gurdon cloned a frog as a way to study embryonic development, interest in cloning technology today is quite different and is focused on four applications. The first involves the cloning of farm animals in such a way that foreign genes are introduce into their cells so they can produce therapeutically useful proteins, such as blood clotting factors to treat hemophilia. Wilmut's team has already cloned animals for this purpose. The second application involves the cloning of livestock to produce a herd of cattle or dairy cows that possess desirable traits. The third application involves a procedure known as therapeutic cloning, whereby human embryos are produced for the purpose of harvesting stem cells, a special kind of cell that may be used to treat many diseases. The fourth application, known as reproductive cloning, involves cloning humans to replace loved ones or to re-create especially talented individuals.

The first two applications of cloning technology are already in progress, but the last two have become extremely controversial and are currently the subject of extensive debate by the general public, legislators, philosophers, and ethicists. Several countries, the United States and the United Kingdom included, have either passed laws to ban reproductive and therapeutic cloning or they are in the process of debating the advisability of such laws. The consensus view would ban reproduction cloning, but such legislation has been difficult to pass, particularly in the United States, where many fear that it will automatically restrict or ban therapeutic cloning.

Human cloning, like human abortion, will be discussed, debated, and argued over for a very long time, and this is as it should be. The issues are complex and extremely important, and although laws may be passed to regulate the technology, society as a whole may never find the legal solutions satisfactory. This is not surprising given some of the questions and speculations that arise when we consider cloning human beings. How many human embryos would a scientist have to sacrifice in order to produce one successful clone? Where are the human embryos for human cloning experiments going to come from, and who will decide how they are to be used? Are cloned farm animals normal, or are they prone to early aging and disease? If they are not normal, should we expect the same for human clones? If a human adult were cloned, would the child be born with its clone-parent's memories, and are they in fact the same person? Does a clone-child have the same legal rights as a natural-born child?

This book, another volume in the New Biology set, discusses all aspects of animal cloning, including the scientific, ethical, and legal issues. Beginning chapters discuss cloning within the context of a natural process that many animals use as a survival strategy, followed by the historical development of the nuclear transfer procedure, the cloning of Dolly the sheep, the medical applications of cloning technology and, finally, the ethical and legal debate. The final chapter provides background material on cell biology, recombinant DNA technology, and other topics that are relevant to animal cloning.

.1.

ALL CLONES
GREAT AND SMALL

Today when we hear the word *clone* we usually think of human beings or farm animals. But most cells, whether living as individuals or as a part of a larger organism, reproduce by cloning themselves. This has always been the case with prokaryotes and is true of many eukaryotes as well. Moreover, cells replace their enzymes by translating the genetic information stored in the DNA and copied into messenger RNA (mRNA). Each time a particular protein is produced, it is identical to previous copies and is, in effect, a clone. The production of proteins in this way is one of nature's most successful cloning experiments.

Scientists can now produce animal clones, but they began by making DNA clones, which form the very heart of biotechnology and paved the way for the birth of Dolly. To understand the full consequences of cloning technology, we must understand what cloning is and how it came to be that nature and scientists have produced such a wide range of clones, from tiny molecules to half-ton dairy cows.

DNA Clones

Just over 100 years ago, biologists were on a roll: Equipped with excellent, high-resolution compound microscopes, and a few histochemical techniques, they were having tremendous success with the identification and treatment of many diseases that were caused by bacteria. Robert Koch, a German country doctor, proved that anthrax, a fatal disease of cattle and humans, is caused by a bacterium, which he named *Bacillus anthracis.* Shortly after Koch's discovery, the great French chemist Louis Pasteur developed a vaccine, the first ever produced to treat anthrax. He quickly followed it up with another vaccine to treat rabies, a disease that was very common in Europe at the time. Paul Ehrlich, who worked in Koch's laboratory, produced a dramatically effective drug, which he called a magic bullet, to treat syphilis. The combined efforts of Koch, Pasteur, and Ehrlich led to treatments for tuberculosis, diphtheria, typhoid fever, and cholera. The knowledge they gained and the techniques they developed transformed the field of medicine from a confused, superstitious muddle into a highly efficient discipline for fighting and controlling infectious diseases.

But knowing how to identify bacteria and how to control them when they become infectious is a long way from understanding how cells do what they do. Basic questions about the cell's genes, molecules, or metabolic pathways drew a complete blank. Not until the 1930s did biochemists begin unraveling some of the details of cellular behavior, but still they knew nothing about the gene's coding for the enzymes they were discovering. They could not even agree on which type of molecule, DNA or protein, was the genetic material. Many scientists believed such questions could never be answered and that our knowledge of the cell would always remain superficial. By 1940 the euphoria of the late 1800s had given way to disappointment, confusion, and a sense of defeat.

The outlook began to brighten in 1952, when Martha Chase and Alfred Hershey proved that DNA, and not protein, is the genetic material of a cell. Their experiment depended on the fact that bacteria, like people, are subject to viral infections. A virus that infects a bacterium is called a bacteriophage, or phage for short. Using the newly developed electron microscopes, other scientists had been able to observe a phage attaching to a bacterial cell, after which the virus, acting like a tiny syringe, injected a long molecule into the bacterium. Within a few hours, phage particles could be seen forming inside the bacteria, after which the cell lysed, or burst open, releasing the newly made daughter phage to infect other bacteria. What did the parental phage inject into the bacteria: protein, DNA, or both? This is the question

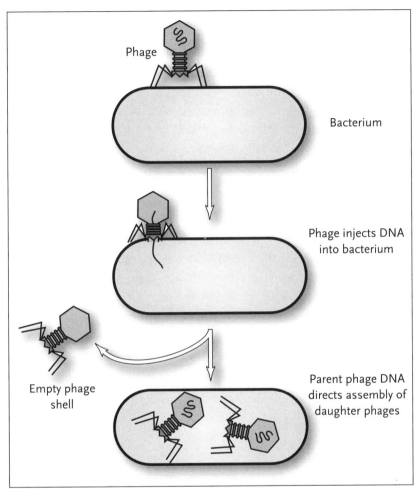

Identifying DNA as genetic material. By labeling the phages, DNA with an isotope of phosphorus and its protein with an isotope of sulfur, Martha Chase and Alfred Hershey were able to show that the phage always injects DNA into the host bacterium.

everyone wanted to answer. In a beautifully elegant experiment, Chase and Hershey showed that the phage always injects DNA into the bacterium, not protein.

With the identity of the cell's genetic material firmly established, many scientists turned their attention to learning more about DNA, and in 1954 James Watson and Francis Crick published a model for the structure of this macromolecule. DNA was shown to be a double helix, consisting of a linear sequence of four different nucleotides encoding the genetic information. In their paper, published in the journal *Nature*, Watson and Crick pointed out that the process of complementary nucleotide pairing provides a simple mechanism for gene duplication prior to cell division (molecules of the cell are described in chapter 8). Within 10 years, other scientists worked out the complete genetic code used by all living cells.

Understanding the molecular nature of the gene reinvigorated the biology community, giving biologists renewed hope that they could answer some of the following questions: How many genes does a prokaryote or a eukaryote have and how are they controlled? Which genes are necessary for the day-to-day running of the cell (the house-keeping genes), and which are needed for embryonic development? Is there a gene for intelligence the way there are genes for eye and hair color? Do cells become cancerous because a gene is not functioning properly, and if so, which one is responsible? The questions are endless, and despite the renewed enthusiasm, most biologists realized it would take a new technology to provide the answers, a technology capable of isolating and amplifying specific genes so their sequence could be deter-mined and their behavior studied in detail. In short, they needed a way to clone DNA molecules.

Throughout the 1960s there was no way to study a gene in detail. DNA encoded the genes in a sequence of nucleotides, but there was no way to determine the exact sequence, nor was it possible to study a gene's activity or expression profile; that is, when it is turned on or off. This began to change in the 1970s with the isolation and purification of protein enzymes that could cut DNA at specific sites and other enzymes that could join two DNA fragments together. These enzymes led the way to the development of recombinant DNA technology that provided methods for cloning specific fragments of DNA (see the Recombinant DNA Primer in chapter 8). Although the development of recombinant technology depended on many brilliant insights into cellular biochem-istry, the cloning of DNA molecules simply takes advantage of the fact that bacteria have been sharing plasmids for millions of years. Indeed, the sharing of molecules is even more ancient than the prokaryotes, extending back to the very first cells, where it may have been crucial for the origin of life.

Cell Clones

Any cell that reproduces asexually is a clone. Bacteria reproduce by binary fission, which is an asexual mode of reproduction. Consequently, bacteria, and indeed all prokaryotes, represent the largest group of clonal organisms on Earth. The fact that bacteria reproduce by cloning themselves seems to be at odds with their amazing adaptability and, in the case of pathogenic bacteria, their ability to develop resistance to antibiotics. A strain of *Staphylococcus aureus* has recently been isolated from a hospital ward that is resistant to all known clinical antibiotics. How can bacteria develop new characteristics such as this when the daughter cells are always genetically identical to the parent cells? How does a daughter cell suddenly become resistant to an antibiotic that would have killed its parent? The answer to these questions lies with the diversity of the prokaryotes, their short 20-minute generation time, and the existence of plasmids.

The Earth contains many different environments, and bacteria of varying species and strains have learned to live in every one of them. Over the short haul, a few days or 10 years, the environment of a particular bacterium is not likely to change much, and for this reason clonal reproduction is not only adequate, it is a wise choice. Over the very long haul, thousands to millions of years, cells do change, whether they clone themselves or not. The DNA of a prokaryote mutates spontaneously at a rate of one nucleotide change every 40 years. The mutation will be inherited by the daughter cell, and if the mutation is useful, the cell will thrive and will pass on to its daughter cell. Bacteria have stayed with this system because, as far as they are concerned, they have all the time in the universe. They are not bothered by the casual mutation rate that is characteristic of asexual reproduction; quite the contrary. With a generation time of only 20 minutes, a useful mutation, when it does occur, can spread throughout a population very quickly.

But the genotype, or genetic composition, of a bacterium is not defined entirely by its main chromosome if it has a plasmid. Plasmids, like the large circular chromosome, carry genes, usually specifying a protein that can destroy or neutralize an antibiotic. Plasmids are released into the environment when bacteria die and can be taken up by other bacteria in the immediate area. Thus, if a bacterium that is sensitive to penicillin happens to acquire a plasmid carrying a penicillin-resistance gene, it can, within minutes, become resistant to the drug.

A clonal creature like a bacterium, striving for regularity and conformity in the short term but equipped with plasmids and a very short generation time, can change dramatically in a surprisingly brief period. With such flexibility, it is not surprising that prokaryotes continue to reproduce in this way. Free living, single-cell eukaryotes known as protozoans also reproduce asexually. Though their reproduction is through the more complex process of mitosis, the final result is the same: two daughter cells, genetically identical to each other. But many protozoans have complex life cycles that alternate between asexual and sexual reproduction. The evolution of sexual reproduction among the protozoans was likely driven by their increased life span, which requires the higher rate of genetic change that sexual reproduction provides.

The situation is somewhat different for eukaryotes that are part of a plant or part of the body of an animal. In the case of an animal's body, all the cells are divided into two kinds: the germ cells and the somatic cells. Germ cells, located in the gonads, divide by meiosis, producing nonidentical daughter cells, or gametes, that are used for sexual reproduction. The somatic cells account for all the rest of the cells in the body. All the somatic cells divide mitotically and make up all the tissues and organs, such as muscle, skin, blood, heart, and kidneys. Consequently, the animal grows through clonal reproduction of the somatic cells but reproduces sexually through the germ cells. Plants have a similar division of cell types. The cells making up the woody part of a rose bush divide asexually so the plant can grow, whereas the germ cells, located in the flower, allow the plant to reproduce sexually.

Animal Clones

Most of the animals that clone themselves are either marine or freshwater invertebrates. This is not to imply that these animals never have sex, since most of them do, but clonal reproduction has become a crucial part of their survival strategy. All these animals are either sessile

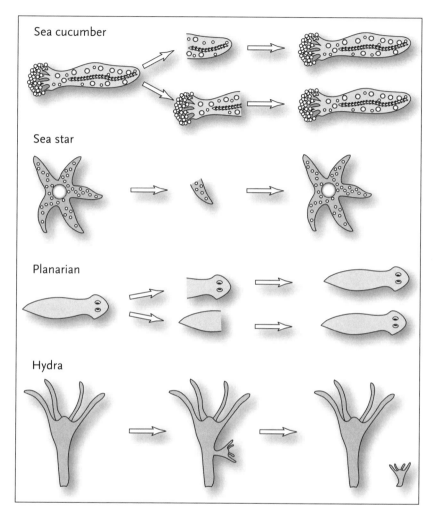

Invertebrate clonal reproduction. Sea cucumbers, sea stars, and planaria can all reproduce asexually by fission or fragmentation. The hydra can clone itself by forming a bud that eventually separates and grows to adult size.

(attached to rocks or ground) or move very slowly. Two echinoderms, the sea cucumbers and the sea stars, are examples of marine invertebrates that reproduce sexually and by cloning themselves. Flatworms (planarian) and the hydra (cnidarian) are their freshwater counterparts. Clonal reproduction also occurs among terrestrial animals, such as the aphid, certain desert lizards, and even among humans.

Sea cucumbers look something like the vegetable they are named after, but ones that are covered in rows of shark's teeth and crowned with a mane of wormlike tentacles. This animal forages on the seabed, where it feeds on detritus; it is affectionately referred to as an ocean-going vacuum cleaner. Being a slow-moving creature, it has to cope with fast-moving predators, a fact that has shaped both the sexual and asexual behavior of this animal. Sexually, sea cucumbers reproduce through a process called broadcast fertilization, whereby the males and females simply release their gametes into the water, where fertilization and development of the embryos and larvae take place.

Broadcast fertilization is a practical method of reproduction for sea cucumbers, since they do not have to spend time finding members of the opposite sex. But there is a major problem with this strategy: The parents cannot protect their offspring, and fish love to eat echinoderm larvae. The sea cucumber tries to compensate by producing millions of larvae, hopefully enough to satisfy the predator's appetite while allowing a few to grow to maturity. If the predation stopped there, sea

Sea cucumber (*Thelonata ananas*) on a sandy seabed. This species of sea cucumber, also known as a prickly redfish, feeds on detritus from the seafloor and may reach a length of up to 70 centimeters. *(SPL/Photo Researchers, Inc.)*

cucumbers could get by well enough with sexual reproduction alone, but unfortunately for them, fish and other predators such as the octopus also love to eat adult sea cucumbers, shark-tooth armor and all.

The survival of the cucumbers depends on the ability of the adults to produce an enormous number of larvae. Even a modest reduction in the size of the adult population can have serious consequences. The cucumbers solved this dilemma by evolving two forms of asexual reproduction: fission and fragmentation. When cucumbers reproduce by fission, they simply break in half, after which both pieces produce complete

The painted sea star (*Orthasterias koehleri*). Found off the coast of Vancouver Island, British Columbia (*Michael Patrick O'Neill/Photo Researchers, Inc.*)

individuals that are genetically identical and therefore are clones of each other. Fragmentation is essentially the same mechanism but one that is initiated by a predator. If a fish or an octopus takes a bite out of a sea cucumber but does not swallow the whole animal, that individual can regenerate itself from the piece that is left behind, as long as it represents at least half the animal's body. Self-cloning has become such an important part of the cucumbers' survival strategy that nearly half of the adults are produced this way.

Sea stars (or starfish) are also capable of asexual reproduction by fragmentation, but they seem to be more efficient at it than the cucumbers. If a predator, such as an octopus, attacks a sea star and eats all of it but a small portion of one arm, that piece of arm can regenerate the entire individual (see the figures on pages 7 and 9). People in the fishing industry first observed the sea star's remarkable talent more than 100 years ago. Starfish were often caught in fishing nets, and it was the custom at the time to cut them up into several pieces before throwing

Light micrograph of the Cnidarian polyp *Hydra*. Other Cnidarians include the jellyfish, sea anemones, and corals. Cnidarians are represented by two body forms: the polyp, which is sedentary, and the medusa, which is free-swimming. *Hydra,* like all Cnidarians, are simple multicellular aquatic animals. The mouth (upper center) is surrounded by tentacles that capture small items of food. These animals can reproduce asexually by budding off a daughter polyp (as seen at left). *(SPL/Photo Researchers, Inc.)*

them overboard. The fishers were hoping to reduce the numbers of starfish in their fishing grounds but abandoned the practice when they noticed it had just the opposite effect. Sea stars, like sea cucumbers, can also reproduce sexually through broadcast fertilization.

Freshwater flatworms can also reproduce through fission or fragmentation to offset losses and damage due to predation. These animals are popular subjects in many research projects aimed at gaining a better understanding of tissue regeneration, with a view to helping people who have lost an arm or a leg. Hydras, another freshwater invertebrate, reproduce asexually through budding. In this case, the clone-daughter first appears as a small outgrowth, or bud, on the surface of the clone-parent, eventually pinching off to live independently. Hydras form buds continually, whether or not a predator has damaged them, but this form of clonal reproduction serves the same adaptive role as fragmentation in sea cucumbers, sea stars, and planarians. If a predator bites off the entire top half of a hydra, the remaining piece of stalk can regenerate the individual. Predation on any of these invertebrates is analogous to the effect on grass of sheep or cattle grazing: As long as they don't consume the entire plant, roots and all, the remainder will grow back. We are all familiar with the regenerative powers of grasses and other plants, but marine and freshwater invertebrates have shown us that simple animals have the same capacity.

For many of the aquatic invertebrates, learning to clone themselves was essential for survival. Echinoderms use it to balance the pressures from their predators to ensure an adequate production of larvae. Asexual reproduction is also important to some aquatic invertebrates as a mechanism of colonization. Hydras are generally sessile, or stationary, creatures, and reproducing asexually is a convenient way for them to colonize a new area. Currents may carry an individual far away from others of its kind, where, if it depended exclusively on sexual reproduction, it would take up the lonely, frustrated existence of an underwater Robinson Crusoe. Self-cloning allows reproduction of an entire population very quickly, and once this is done, many of these animals will revert to sexual reproduction.

Terrestrial invertebrates, of which insects and spiders are the sole representatives, reproduce sexually, but this is not their only form of reproduction. Some, like the aphids, have a complex life cycle that includes both sexual and asexual reproduction. These insects are small (about 2 mm long), usually green or yellow in color, and are found feeding on nearly all indoor and outdoor ornamental plants, as well as vegetables, field crops, and fruit trees.

Aphids spend the winter as fertilized eggs attached to stems

Aphids (*Acyrtosiphon*) being preyed upon by a ladybug (*Harmonia congoblata*). Aphids clone themselves through parthenogenesis. *(Nigel Cattlin/Photo Researchers, Inc.)*

or other parts of plants. The young insects (or nymphs) hatch from these eggs and mature into wingless females called stem mothers. Males appear later in the year. Stem mothers reproduce by parthenogenesis (eggs and embryos are produced mitotically, without mating), and the eggs are held within their bodies until they hatch, so that nymphs are born alive. All offspring are females, which soon mature and begin to reproduce in the same manner. This asexual portion of the life cycle may last for more than a dozen generations. Eventually, some or all of the young aphids develop wings and migrate to other plants. As autumn approaches, bringing with it shorter days and cooler temperatures, a generation appears that includes both males and females. After mating, these females lay fertilized eggs to complete the cycle.

Aphids, like sea cucumbers and hydras, clone themselves, but their reason for doing so is quite different. When an aphid is caught by one of its predators, such as the ladybug, it is killed and consumed with no parts left behind, so there is no point in trying to exploit the properties of fragmentation. Instead, this little insect uses clonal reproduction to maximize the availability of food for its young. The stem mothers are, in effect, born pregnant so no time is wasted in a search for sexual partners, egg development, and so forth. As soon as the vegetation is in bloom, the aphid population is there, ready and waiting. And since most of the other insects reproduce sexually, there will be a brief period when the aphids have the fresh vegetation all to themselves, usually to the dismay of the family gardener or farmer.

Most vertebrates, whether aquatic or terrestrial, reproduce sexually, but there are some that prefer to clone themselves. When animals began roaming the Earth, many of them learned to live in extremely harsh but stable environments. Some species spent millions of years fine-tuning their anatomy and physiology so they could live in a desert or on the ice floes of Antarctica. Among this unusually hardy group of animals is the whiptail lizard, living in the deserts of the southwestern United States. To look at them, you would think whiptails are very ordinary lizards, but on closer inspection, two things become evident: First, they all look remarkably alike, and second, they are all females. Whiptails, like aphids, reproduce by parthenogenesis, but their life cycle does not include a sexual stage, nor do males ever appear in the population. How this came to be is not clear. Perhaps the number of whiptails dropped so low that the males and females had trouble finding each other. Somehow females appeared in the population that could reproduce asexually, and eventually the male line died out. Presumably, these females were exceptionally well adapted to their environment, so the loss of sexual reproduction was no disadvantage.

However, relying entirely on asexual reproduction is a practical strategy only when the environment is stable. Deserts rarely revert to wetlands, and the whiptails are betting they never will. However, most environments are not so stable, and for this reason, other creatures that clone themselves, like sea cucumbers or aphids, retain the ability to reproduce sexually in order to guard against the possibility of entering a genetic dead-end and the threat of imminent extinction that comes with it.

Twins Are Natural Clones

Mammals, such as ourselves, our farm animals, and our pets use sex to reproduce, and in the natural environment there are no exceptions. But this is not to say that we never clone ourselves; we do, but we call it twinning instead of cloning. Identical twins occur when the two-cell embryo splits into two separate cells, or blastomeres, both of which develop into a normal adult, with each being the clone of the other.

Scientists would now like to extend this natural process to the cloning of adults. The reasons for doing so are sometimes vague, but in the case of farm animals, the intention is to produce herds of genetically identical individuals very quickly, or to use cloning as a way to produce transgenic animals that function as pharmaceutical factories or serve as a convenient source of vital organs. Those wishing to clone human adults usually cite a desire to replace a loved one or to create copies of gifted individuals.

Needless to say, the prospect of scientists cloning human adults has stirred up a bit of controversy. We mammals are sexual creatures and tend to take a dim view of any attempt to short-circuit the process. We seem to have an intuitive grasp on nature's love for variability, and it is no accident that the most intelligent creatures on this planet are mammals: creatures that not only reproduce sexually but also spend a great deal of time nurturing and caring for their young. Our full range of emotions and our intelligence can be traced to the nurturing that is typical of mammals. Our sense of suffering, and the pain we feel when a loved one is hurt or killed, has molded our psyches and was there the first time an early human picked up a stick to drive off a predator or when scientists developed the first vaccine that saved children dying from diphtheria. In the face of cloning, it is our humanity that we fear to lose.

.2.

A HISTORY OF CLONING EXPERIMENTS

Experimental cloning began in an attempt to understand embryonic development. Plants and animals, in honor of their very distant ancestors, begin life as a single cell. We call that cell an egg or an oocyte, and when the oocyte is fertilized, a developmental program is activated that produces an organism made up of many millions, sometimes billions, of cells. But the creation of a multicellular creature is not just a matter of an oocyte dividing many times to produce a great bunch of cells. Instead, embryogenesis is a combination of cellular division and differentiation. Cell division increases the number of cells, while differentiation transforms those cells into many different kinds. By the time a human infant is born, the child's body consists of several billion cells, representing 200 distinct types that form our flesh and blood.

Cellular differentiation is clearly evident in the physical transformation of the embryo throughout development. Embryonic development is similar in most animal species and is divided into three major stages: The first stage is the formation of a blastula, a spherical hollow ball of embryonic cells known as blastomeres. The second stage occurs when the blastula invaginates to produce a gastrula, which defines the body axis and establishes future identities of the cells and tissue layers. The final stage begins with the formation of a nervous system and, in the case of vertebrates, the segmented spinal column. At this stage, the embryo is called a neurula, and the process is known as neurulation. The final form of an embryo also depends on organogenesis, or the formation of organs such as the heart and kidneys, and morphogenesis, whereby

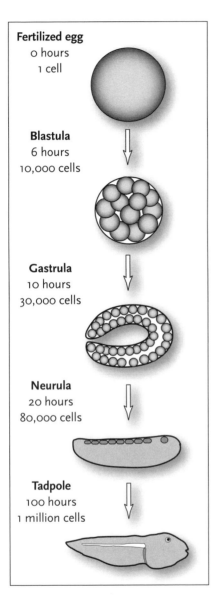

Fertilized egg
o hours
1 cell

Blastula
6 hours
10,000 cells

Gastrula
10 hours
30,000 cells

Neurula
20 hours
80,000 cells

Tadpole
100 hours
1 million cells

Embryonic development in the frog. The fertilized egg divides to produce a hollow ball of cells called a blastula, which invaginates to form a gastrula. Development of the nervous system and a segmented spinal column produces a neurula. The tadpole eventually forms into an adult frog after going through a nonembryonic stage called metamorphosis.

similar tissues are molded into different structures, such as an arm and a leg.

Embryos Inspire the First Cloning Experiment

While Louis Pasteur was using his microscope to study bacteria, other biologists were using their instruments to study embryonic development, and they quickly realized that cellular differentiation posed a major riddle: How can a single cell, the oocyte, with one genome differentiate into so many different kind of cells? If all the cells have the same genes, why don't they all look and act alike? In 1885, August Weismann, a German zoologist, proposed that embryonic development was associated with a diminution, or loss, of genes. Brain cells become brain cells because they have lost the genes specifying liver or skin but retain genes that specify neurons. Weismann further suggested that diminution began with the first cell division, in which the left blastomere retained genes for the left side of the embryo and the right blastomere had only genes for the right side. With the first division of the egg, all the cells lost their totipotency; that is, they could no longer give rise to a complete individual.

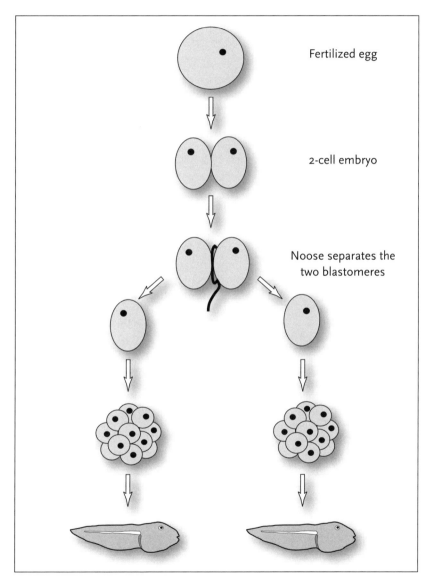

Fertilized egg

2-cell embryo

Noose separates the two blastomeres

Experiment to test totipotency. A noose was used to separate a two-cell embryo into two blastomeres. Development proceeded normally in both embryos, proving that nuclei at the two-cell stage are totipotent.

Two other German embryologists, Wilhelm Roux and Hans Dreisch, set out to test Weismann's theory shortly after it was proposed. Roux collected fertilized eggs of the frog, *Rana esculenta;* as soon as an egg divided, producing a two-cell embryo, he destroyed one of the blastomeres by poking it with a hot needle. Roux reasoned that if the two blastomeres retained the same genetic information, the undamaged one would develop normally, but if diminution occurred, as Weismann predicted, it would not. Each time Roux performed his experiment, the embryo failed to develop normally and Weismann's theory seemed to have been confirmed. Hans Dreisch was not convinced, however, and in 1894 he decided to try a similar experiment using sea urchin embryos. Instead of destroying one blastomere, the way Roux had done, he shook the two-cell embryo until it separated into two cells, both of which developed normally. Dreisch concluded that Weismann was wrong and that Roux's experiments were flawed: Perhaps destroying one blastomere damaged the other or prevented it from developing normally. But Dreisch was unable to repeat his experiment using frog embryos, as they would not shake apart, and he could find no way of separating the two blastomeres without damaging one or both of them.

Dr. Hans Spemann, a 19th-century German embryologist who performed the first animal cloning experiment using amphibian embryos *(Courtesy of the National Library of Medicine)*

Hans Spemann, a German scientist with a passion for embryology, was finishing his Ph.D. when Dreisch was conducting his experiments. Although Dreisch could not separate amphibian blastomeres, Spemann developed a simple and elegant method to separate the cells without damaging either one. After collecting fertilized salamander eggs, he very carefully, and with infinite patience, looped a strand of a hair taken from his newborn son between the two blastomeres and gently tightened the noose until the

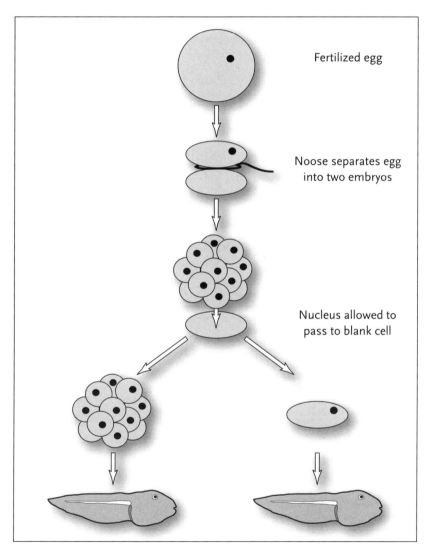

The first cloning experiment. A noose was tied around a fertilized salamander egg to produce one cell with a nucleus and one without (blank cell). At the 16-cell stage, the noose was loosened to allow a nucleus to pass into the blank cell, after which the 16-cell embryo was separated from the one-cell embryo.

two cells came apart. Both of the blastomeres went on to produce normal tadpoles.

Spemann concluded that nuclei at the two-cell stage are totipotent. Weismann's diminution, as Dreisch had shown, did not occur. But, Spemann wondered, was it possible that diminution occurred more gradually? Are nuclei at a more advanced stage still totipotent? To answer these questions, Spemann performed a second test of totipotency, which is also the first cloning experiment using nuclear transfer ever conducted. Again, Spemann collected fertilized salamander eggs, but this time he did not wait for them to divide. Instead, he quickly tied a loop of baby hair around the egg and gently tightened the noose to produce two blastomeres, one with a nucleus and one without (an enucleated, or blank, cell). He kept the noose tightened until the nucleated blastomere divided to produce 16 cells, at which time he loosened the noose just enough to let a nucleus from the 16-cell embryo pass into the blank cell. Quickly, he tightened the noose and kept it drawn until the 16-cell embryo separated from the one-cell embryo, and to his delight, both went on to develop into normal tadpoles.

Spemann was a very thorough scientist who devoted his entire professional life to the study of embryos. Throughout his career he conducted many experiments, some of which earned him, along with his brilliant student, Hilde Mangold, the Nobel Prize. He was amazed, and to some extent overwhelmed, by the complexity and level of integration that he observed in developing embryos, but the question of totipotency was always on his mind. In 1938 he wrote *Embryonic Development and Induction,* in which he wondered if cell nuclei remained totipotent throughout the life span of the adult. What would happen, he asked, if a nucleus from an adult cell were transferred into an enucleated egg? He did not call it "cloning" but referred to it as a "fantastical experiment." Spemann was excited about this experiment but could see no way of conducting it, and indeed, it would take more than 50 years before anyone could find a way to do it. When they did, Weismann's theory was laid to rest, once and for all.

Cloning Frogs Is a Partial Success

Robert Briggs and his graduate student, Thomas King, cloned the first frog in 1952 at a research institute in Philadelphia. This was not quite the "fantastical experiment" envisioned by Spemann. Briggs and King obtained their nucleus from a gastrula, not an adult, but it was an important first step. Using extremely fine pipettes, King withdrew the nucleus from a frog's egg (oocyte), in this case *Rana pipens,* then injected a nucleus from a gastrula into the now-enucleated oocyte. The embryo developed normally up to the tadpole stage, at which time the experiment was declared a success, even though the researchers had not waited for the tadpole to metamorphose into an adult. They repeated their experiment many times, eventually cloning 27 tadpoles from a total of 197 oocytes that had received a transplanted gastrula nucleus. They found, however, that their success rate dropped dramatically when they tried to use nuclei from a neurula, a later-stage embryo. Briggs and King eventually concluded that Weismann was at least partially correct. Nuclei from older embryos did not appear to be totipotent. Perhaps, they thought, the DNA was somehow rearranged during development so that the cells pass a point of no return. If true, this meant it would never be possible to clone an adult.

John Gurdon, at Cambridge University, felt the problem was not that cells lost their totipotency but that it was being repressed. The genes are all there, but the oocyte cannot use them. Cloning an adult would require reconditioning the adult cell nucleus so it could support embryonic development. Gurdon also suspected that the damage done to the oocytes, while having their nuclei removed, might have contributed to the failure Briggs and King encountered when trying to clone from older embryos.

But Gurdon was not interested in cloning an embryo. Briggs and King had already done that. Instead, he set out to clone an adult frog, and he chose to work on the African toad, *Xenopus laevis,* because the species has especially large, clear eggs. Clear eggs were important because rather than withdrawing the oocyte nucleus with a pipette, as Briggs and King had done, Gurdon destroyed it with ultraviolet (UV) radiation. He then collected epithelial cells from the intestinal tract of an adult toad and placed them in tissue culture. As soon as an oocyte was exposed to UV, it received another nucleus obtained from the cultured epithelial cells. In some cases, after the clone developed to the blastula or gastrula stage, its nuclei were isolated and injected into other oocytes in an attempt to recondition them through another round of cloning.

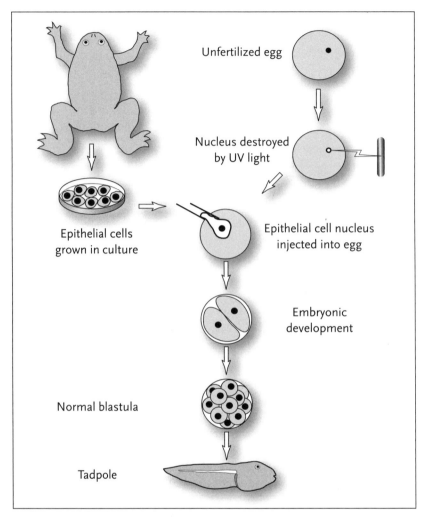

Cloning a frog by nuclear transfer. Epithelial cells are collected from an adult and grown in culture. An unfertilized egg cell is collected and exposed to UV radiation to destroy its nucleus. A nucleus, with some cytoplasm surrounding it, is extracted from a cultured epithelial cell and injected into the enucleated egg. If successful, the clone will develop into a normal blastula and finally a tadpole.

After several rounds of this treatment, it was assumed that the nuclei were reprogrammed and could support full development, right up to the adult stage.

Many of Gurdon's experiments led to the production of cloned tadpoles, a few of which metamorphosed into adult frogs. However, shortly after he published his results, other scientists discovered stems cells in the intestinal tract of *Xenopus,* casting some doubt on the outcome of the experiment. Stems cells are undifferentiated and account for about 2.5 percent of the cell population in the gut lining. If nuclei from these cells were used, Gurdon's experiment would be more like cloning an embryo rather than an adult. Moreover, Gurdon's success rate for obtaining cloned adults was about 2 percent, very close to the expected proportion of stem cells in his tissue culture samples.

Nevertheless, Gurdon's success, partial though it was, made it clear to most scientists that cells retained their totipotency and that it was only a matter of time before someone found a way to rewaken a differentiated nucleus so that an adult animal could be cloned.

Cloning Mammals Is Declared Impossible

Gurdon's work was both exciting and exasperating. Cloning an adult could be done, many were certain of it, but so far no one had been able to do it. And when discussions came around to the possibility of using nuclear transfer to clone a mammal, everyone seemed to think it would be impossible. First of all, frog embryos develop in the water, so the mother frog stocks her eggs with everything the embryos will need to grow, and for this reason their eggs are very large, making them relatively easy to work with. In addition, because development of the embryo occurs outside the mother's body, frog eggs that are being prepared for a cloning experiment can simply be returned to the water for incubation, with few special precautions needed.

Mammalian embryos, on the other hand, get their nourishment from the mother through the placenta, so there is no need for the eggs to be stocked with food reserves the way frogs' eggs are. This is why a mammalian egg is so tiny, only $1/_{100}$ the size of a frog's egg. In addition, the placenta is derived from the trophoblast, an opaque cell layer that surrounds the embryo, making manipulations of the embryonic cells extremely difficult. The trophoblast also gives rise to the chorion, a membrane that surrounds the embryo, forming a safe, fluid-filled chamber in which development occurs. The placenta and chorion can develop only in a mother's womb. Mammalian eggs, after being manipulated in a cloning experiment, cannot simply be placed in a fluid-filled culture dish for the embryo to develop. Instead, they have to be implanted in the womb of a surrogate mother that will carry the embryo to term. All these conditions made the cloning of mammals seem impossible.

But there are always scientists around who enjoy attempting the impossible, and in 1981, Karl Illmensee and his associate Peter Hoppe reported cloning three mice. Again, this was not Spemann's "fantastical experiment," since Illmensee obtained nuclei from embryonic, not adult, mouse cells, but it was, nevertheless, a stunning achievement. Illmensee used the basic procedures for nuclear transfer, established in the earlier frog cloning experiments, as well as techniques for handling mammalian oocytes that were developed in the 1970s by Patrick Steptoe and Robert Edwards for in vitro fertilization (that is, fertilization in a culture dish) of human embryos.

Illmensee and Hoppe collected fertilized eggs from black

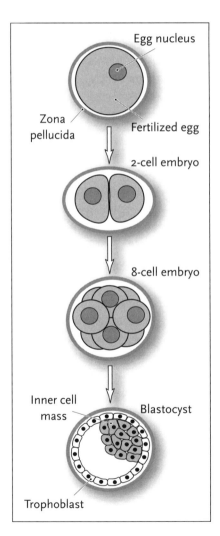

Mammalian embryogenesis up to the blastula stage. Mammalian embryos, unlike amphibians, are surrounded by nonembryonic cells that make up the zona pellucida and trophoblast, the latter giving rise to the placenta and chorionic membrane. The embryonic cells are in the inner cell mass.

mice and developing embryos from gray and brown-colored mice. Nuclei were isolated from the embryos and injected into the eggs, after which the egg's original nuclei were removed using the same pipette. After the cloned embryos were constructed, they were allowed to grow in vitro for a few days before being implanted in the uterus of white surrogate mothers. Three apparently healthy mice were born. One was brown and the other two were gray. The coat color provided an immediate confirmation that the genetic origin of these mice was the nuclei obtained from gray and brown embryos.

The real power of science lies in the fact that it is based on experimentation and the careful description of the experimental method, so other scientists can try to replicate the results. Experiments that cannot be replicated, or repeated with the same results, are of little use to anyone and cannot help us gain a better understanding of nature. Indeed, when scientists are unable to replicate an experiment, they tend to get rather grumpy about it and usually conclude that the procedure is faulty or that the scientists responsible for developing the experimental protocol are less than reputable. Perhaps they simply did not get the results they claimed.

This was the situation facing Illmensee and Hoppe soon after they published the results of their cloning experiment, for others tried to replicate their results but were unable to do so. Some scientists went so far as to assert that the results were not only fraudulent but also that the cloning of mammals was biologically impossible.

Cloning Farm Animals Settles the Debate

Scientists, like everyone else, occasionally get the wind knocked out of their sails. Illmensee and Hoppe's cloning experiments were greeted with great enthusiasm, but eventually the careers of both scientists were ruined by the suspicion that their results were fraudulent. Not everyone believed this, however. Nor did everyone think that cloning a mammal was impossible; they believed in Mark Twain's observation that you can't depend on your eyes when your imagination is out of focus. And indeed, in 1986, just five years after Illmensee's trouble began, Steen Willadsen, working in Cambridge, England, cloned a sheep from embryonic cells.

Willadsen, a veterinarian turned reproductive biologist, began by finding ways to freeze and store sheep embryos. This is important because many embryos are usually required for these studies, and it is necessary to collect as many as possible during the breeding season, after which they are stored until needed. After thawing some of his embryos, Willadsen transferred them to surrogate mothers, and eventually he was able to get healthy lambs and calves from embryos that had been frozen and stored.

He then decided to try a simple twinning experiment, using Spemann's method to separate a two-cell sheep embryo into two healthy blastomeres. But the procedure is not as straightforward with mammalian embryos as it is with amphibians. Splitting a two-cell mammalian embryo destroys the zona pellucida, without which the embryo cannot be reared in vitro. In Spemann's experiment, the split blastomeres were placed in pond water for development to continue. With mammalian embryos, it is necessary to incubate them in vitro for a day or two before implanting them in a surrogate mother. The in vitro step is carried out in the fallopian tubes of a rabbit, either in situ (still intact in the rabbit) or isolated and kept alive in a culture dish. In either case, without the protection of the zona pellucida, the rabbit's immune cells quickly destroy the embryo. Willadsen solved this problem by coating the separated blastomeres in a gelatinous substance called agar before placing them in the fallopian tubes. Nutritive molecules, being supplied by the fallopian tubes, can pass through the agar, but the cells of the immune system cannot. After three to four days the individual blastomeres, now grown to 16-cell embryos, were transferred to a surrogate mother, where they developed into healthy twins.

Having perfected his technique with twinning experiments, Willadsen cloned three sheep from an eight-cell embryo and then extended his experiments to dairy cows, which he cloned from more advanced, and more highly differentiated, embryos consisting of 120 cells. These experiments set the stage for Spemann's "fantastical experiment," the cloning of a sheep named Dolly from adult cells. It was not until Dolly's birth, in 1996, that Weismann's theory was finally laid to rest. Genes are not lost during development but simply repressed, and thus embryonic development occurs through a process of differential gene expression.

That is, turning genes on or off in a way that is specific to each cell type. All the cells in an adult's body express the basic housekeeping genes, but liver cells do not express brain-specific genes, and neurons do not express liver-specific genes.

·3·
A CLONE NAMED DOLLY

When Dolly was born, on July 5, 1996, Hans Spemann's fantastical experiment was finally accomplished. But Spemann was not on Ian Wilmut's mind when he set out to clone sheep. Most biologists, including Wilmut, knew about Spemann and the work of Illmensee and Willadsen, but scientists often end up going down a particular research trail simply because it is the only one open at that moment in time. In some cases, they may have been hired to solve a particular problem and, in trying to deal with it, ended up on a path that happens to run parallel to the research efforts of other scientists.

Dr. Ian Wilmut, a British scientist at the Roslin Institute in Scotland, who led the team that cloned Dolly the sheep from an adult cell. *(SPL/Photo Researchers, Inc.)*

Research is, after all, an exploration of the unknown, one that plays out like an old-fashioned detective story, where each bit of information becomes a clue that leads to the next piece in the puzzle. Scientists, like all good bloodhounds, simply follow the nose. From time to time, they also consult their intellect, and if they are wise they hope for a bit of luck. Nonscientists are often surprised to hear this. They assume a researcher approaches a problem in a very organized, systematic fashion: Form a hypothesis, conduct the experiment, analyze the data, draw the conclusions, and paint the final picture. Deductive reasoning plays a big part in all this, but as likely as not, it is intuitive insight and plain old dumb luck that save the day. Scientists generally shy away from the phrase "dumb luck," preferring to call it serendipity.

Serendipity played a major role in the birth of Dolly. Ian Wilmut did not set out to prove the biology community wrong in its assertion that the cloning of mammals was biologically impossible, nor was he trying to fulfill Spemann's dream. He was simply trying to find a better way to produce transgenic farm animals, and along the way, he and his team accidentally hit upon the importance of G_0. Without that piece of the puzzle, Dolly would have remained a dream.

Dolly Is Cloned from an Adult Cell

The totipotency of cell nuclei declines as an embryo develops into an adult. Before Dolly's birth, the question of whether it is possible to reprogram a fully differentiated nucleus had never been resolved. So the birth of Dolly came as quite a shock to scientists around the world, because the nucleus that was used to produce her came from a fully differentiated mammary gland cell that was originally obtained from a six-year-old poll Dorset ewe.

Poll Dorsets are a common Scottish breed of sheep that are all white. Another popular breed is the Scottish blackface, which is very similar to a poll Dorset, except that it is larger and, of course, has a black face. Both breeds figured prominently in the experiments that led to Dolly. A poll Dorset has a life span of about 12 years, so the cell that gave rise to Dolly was not only from an adult but a middle-aged adult at that. Dolly, being derived from a poll Dorset nucleus, is herself a member of this breed.

The general scheme for cloning Dolly involves placing a nucleus from an ovine mammary gland epithelial (OME) cell into an enucleated egg obtained from a Scottish blackface. Steen Willadsen originally introduced the nuclear transfer procedure that Wilmut and Campbell

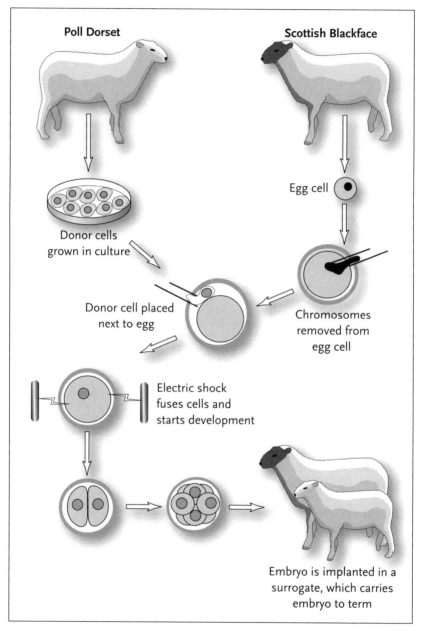

How to clone a sheep. The poll Dorset provides the nucleus, which is obtained from cultured ovine mammary gland epithelial (OME) cells. The blackface provides the egg, which is subsequently enucleated. If the cloning process is successful, the clone will look like a poll Dorset.

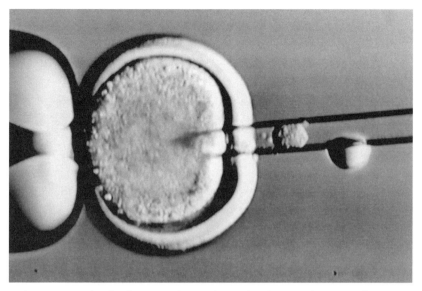

Light micrograph of a sheep egg being injected with an embryonic cell during sheep cloning *(SPL/Photo Researchers, Inc.)*

used. The karyoplast (the cell donating the nucleus) is injected into the space between the zona pellucida and egg cell. The karyoplast and the cytoplast (the enucleated egg) are then fused together with an electric current. This is a much gentler procedure, compared to injecting the nucleus into the egg by poking another hole in the egg's membrane (the first hole was made when the egg's chromosomes were removed). Once development begins, the embryo is encased in agar and incubated temporarily in the oviduct of a blackface (not shown in the figure), after which it is transferred to the oviduct of the final surrogate mother, also a blackface, which carries it to term.

Wilmut and his team constructed a total of 277 embryos, of which 29 developed to the blastocyst stage in the temporary surrogate. These blastocysts were removed from the agar and transferred to 13 blackface ewes, one of which became pregnant and gave birth to Dolly. With only one out of 277 embryos going full term, it is a wonder the experiment worked at all. The scientists could tell at a glance that the experiment had worked, since Dolly was clearly a whiteface poll Dorset and not a Scottish blackface. Despite the obvious differences between the surrogate mother and Dolly, extensive DNA tests were conducted to prove that Dolly's genome came from the culture of OME cells, and that she was indeed a clone of one of those cells.

The Importance of Being G_0

Why was Wilmut's team successful when so many before them had failed? When we compare the figure on p. 30 with the figure on p. 22 (the frog cloning experiments), we notice that in broad outline, they are very similar procedures. But there are many differences between the experiments that led to a cloned frog and those that produced Dolly. The gentle fusion of the karyoplast to the cytoplast and the coating of the embryo in agar for the pre-incubation period were important innovations, but the crucial difference between the Dolly experiment and all other previous cloning experiments is the consideration Wilmut's team paid to the details of the cell cycle (the cell cycle is described in chapter 8).

One of Dr. Wilmut's team members, Dr. Keith Campbell, a specialist in cell-cycle control mechanisms, realized that the chances of successfully cloning a sheep would be much greater if the cells being used as nuclear donors were in G_0. There are two reasons for this: First, the chromatin of a G_0 nucleus is especially susceptible to reprogramming, and second, the nucleus is still diploid. If the cell has been allowed to pass through S phase and into G_2, the DNA has duplicated, producing a tetraploid nucleus. Failure is guaranteed if such a nucleus is transferred into an enucleated egg.

Mammalian eggs released at ovulation are in metaphase of meiosis II; that is, they have passed through meiosis I and, with the completion of meiosis II, will become haploid. When the sperm enters an egg, it stimulates the completion of meiosis II, activating development. An important part of activation is the joining of the egg nucleus with the sperm nucleus to reconstitute a normal diploid nucleus. This is the reason cloning experiments using nuclei from G_2 or S cells fail: the egg is expecting to begin development with a diploid nucleus but finds itself trying to deal with one that is tetraploid, or nearly so. Total confusion results, and the embryo dies.

Campbell devised a simple method for ensuring the cells used to obtain nuclei were in G_0. First, the cells were grown in culture, then certain growth factors were left out when the culture medium was changed. Cells that were in G_1 left the cycle and entered G_0. Cells that were in S phase or G_2 either died or entered G_0 after completing their cycle. After a time it could be safely assumed that all of the cells were in G_0 and could be used as a source of donor nuclei. Initially, it was believed that G_1 and G_0 were equivalent, since the nucleus is diploid in either stage, but Campbell quickly realized that G_0 was not just a resting stage. Several lines of evidence provided by other scientists showed that this stage of the cell cycle was associated with subtle changes in chromatin structure, making the nucleus much easier to reprogram.

Campbell also considered the cell cycle stage of the oocyte and the possible effects it might have on reprogramming G_0 nuclei. All mammalian oocytes develop through meiosis I and stop at metaphase of meiosis II, at which point the duplicated chromosomes, held together at the centromeres, are lined up along the spindle. If they are never fertilized, they never complete meiosis. They are, in a sense, locked in a form of suspended animation, a condition that is controlled by maturation-promoting factor (MPF). MPF is responsible for triggering chromosome condensation and the breakdown of the nuclear envelope. MPF is, in turn, regulated by a molecule called CSF. When a sperm enters an egg, it triggers an influx of calcium ions into the cell. The calcium blocks CSF, leading to a drop in MPF activity. With MPF gone, the chromosomes decondense, the nuclear envelope reforms, and the cell completes meiosis II. Thus it is the influx of calcium that activates development, not sperm entry. Consequently, it is possible to add a nucleus to an egg without activating it, simply by carrying out the procedure in a solution that lacks calcium. In addition, adding a nucleus to an egg without activation would expose the nucleus to high levels of MPF, which could help reprogram the transplanted nucleus.

These facts were used to design three cloning protocols, referred to as MAGIC, GOAT, and UNIVERSAL, all of which use G_0 nuclei:

> *MAGIC (metaphase arrested G_0-accepting cytoplast)*   The karyoplast, the cell donating the nucleus, is fused to the cytoplast (the enucleated egg) in calcium-free solution. Four to six hours later development is stimulated with another electric shock, this time in a solution containing calcium. The MAGIC protocol exposes

the G_0 nucleus to the potential reprogramming environment provided by high MPF levels.

GOAT (G_0 activation and transfer)   In this case, fusion of the karyoplast and cytoplast occurs simultaneously with the electric shock. This procedure most accurately reflects normal conception. MPF

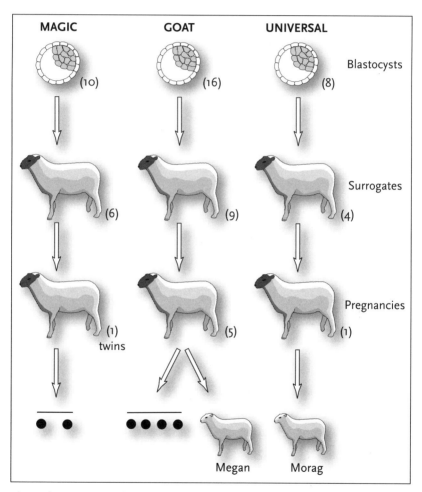

Three cloning protocols. The MAGIC, GOAT, and UNIVERSAL protocols were tested in a series of experiments that produced Megan and Morag, the first mammals cloned from cultured, embryonic cells. The number of embryos and fetuses at each stage are shown in parentheses. The black dots indicate the lamb was born dead, or died, soon after birth.

levels begin dropping as soon as the cytoplast is activated, so the G_0 nucleus is exposed to high levels of MPF for only a brief moment.

UNIVERSAL   An electric shock activates the cytoplast, and four to six hours later the karyoplast is added. Consequently, G_0 nucleus is never exposed to MPF, which will have disappeared by the time fusion occurs. This protocol is called "universal" because eggs without MPF were thought capable of accepting nuclei in any stage of the cell cycle.

Wimut's team tested these protocols before the Dolly experiment, and they resulted in the live birth of two sheep, Megan and Morag. The birth of these two sheep marked the first time a mammal had been cloned from cultured cells; the cells used were obtained from sheep embryos that had been kept in culture for a month or two. Steen Willadsen had previously cloned sheep from embryonic cells but not from cells that had been placed in culture. The difference is important. Cloning from cultured cells is much more difficult because the cells have had a chance to differentiate, and their nuclei must be reprogrammed.

Dolly was cloned from an adult cell kept in culture for several months using the GOAT protocol. The choice of this protocol rested primarily on the fact that it produced the greatest number of pregnancies, even though it yielded only one live birth (Megan). The preliminary experiments involving Megan and Morag simply had too few embryos going to full term for a clear distinction to be made between MAGIC, GOAT, and UNIVERSAL. Theoretically, MAGIC should have been the best and UNIVERSAL the worst protocol. The GOAT protocol was a happy compromise, in that it produced a live birth and exposed the transplanted nucleus to MPF for a time, brief though it was.

The careful attention to the details of the cell cycles of both the egg and donor nucleus cell is widely accepted as the crucial element in the Dolly experiment, but the difficulty of reprogramming an adult nucleus is evident from the large number of embryos that were produced, from which only one live birth, Dolly, resulted. With only one out of 277 cloned embryos carried to term, it is not surprising that the experiments of other scientists, who ignored the details of the cell cycle, failed, producing the false conclusion that the cloning of mammals is biologically impossible. Cloning mammals is not impossible, just extremely difficult.

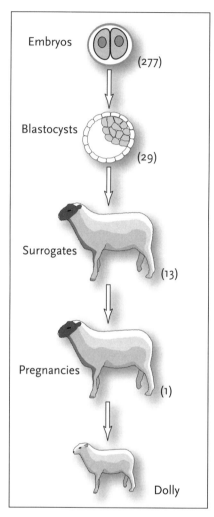

Embryos (277)

Blastocysts (29)

Surrogates (13)

Pregnancies (1)

Dolly

The Dolly experiment. Dolly was cloned from an adult mammary gland cell via the GOAT protocol. The difficulty of reprogramming adult nuclei is apparent from the very large number of embryos produced, from which only a single lamb, Dolly, was born.

Cloning from Cultured Cells

Dolly was not just the first mammal cloned from an adult cell; she was also the first mammal cloned from adult cells grown in culture. Obtaining nuclei from cultured cells converts cloning from an interesting experiment to an extremely powerful method for producing transgenic animals. This was in fact Ian Wilmut's primary interest from the very beginning.

Transgenic animals are those that have had a foreign gene introduced into their genome by a process called transfection. Prior to Dolly's birth, the only method available for producing transgenic animals was to inject individual embryos with the foreign gene, after which the researchers had to wait for the birth of the animal before they could confirm the success of the experiment. Transfecting cells in culture is simpler, more effective, and more efficient. In some cases, it is only necessary to add the foreign gene to the culture medium, after which the cells will take it up and incorporate it into their genome. This is analogous to plasmid swapping, something that prokaryotes have been doing since life appeared on this planet.

Transfecting cells in culture offers a second, equally important advantage over previous methods: The cells may be tested to confirm the uptake and proper expression of the foreign gene before they are used in a cloning experiment. Some cells may incorporate the foreign gene but express it at levels too low to be of any use. By using standard molecular procedures, scientists can screen millions of transfected cells for the expression of the foreign gene. Once this is done, cells producing the desired amount can be isolated for cloning experiments. Using this approach, female sheep can be cloned that produce large quantities of valuable proteins in their milk. In 1997, Wilmut's team cloned a transgenic sheep named Polly that carries the human gene for blood clotting factor IX. This important protein can now be produced in large quantities to treat hemophiliacs.

Dolly's Life and Death

By all accounts, Dolly was a healthy sheep right up to her death, at the age of six, on February 14, 2003. Dolly gave birth to six healthy lambs (one in 1998, two in 1999, and triplets in 2000). When she was born, many scientists feared she might develop a variety of medical disorders because all her cells have abnormally short telomeres. Telomere length decreases as cells divide; the cell used to clone Dolly came from a six-year-old sheep and had been kept in cell culture for many weeks. At birth, Dolly's genome was already middle-aged.

Wilmut's team analyzed Dolly's telomeres in 2000 and showed that they were indeed about 20 percent shorter than is normal for a poll Dorset of Dolly's age. But the damaging effects of shortened telomeres on the health of a cell and the physiology of the organism are still highly speculative. In 2001, Dolly was reported to have developed arthritis in her left knee and hip joint. Arthritis is a common ailment in sheep, although it usually affects other joints. There is no way to know if the arthritis was related to the length of her telomeres or to the fact that she was a clone, simply because there are too few clones available for the information to be meaningful.

Other cloned animals do seem to suffer from a variety of medical problems. Dairy cows cloned in 2001 suffer from immune deficiencies. Two of three cloned Charolais calves, also cloned in 2001, died of an intestinal infection caused by a depressed immune system. The three calves, cloned at the California State University at Chico, were the only survivors among more than two dozen fertilized eggs planted in surrogate mothers. The success rate for the Dolly experiment was even lower and could also have been caused by problems with the immune system.

Researchers involved in animal cloning are actively monitoring their clones for subtle physiological abnormalities. Some abnormalities are likely to occur among the few cloned individuals that make it to adulthood. Scientists at the Roslin Institute estimate that a cloned fetus is 10 times more likely to die in utero than a fetus produced by normal sexual means. This state of affairs will not change until scientists gain a better understanding of nuclear reprogramming. When this happens, it may be possible to improve the success rate for cloning sheep from the current 1–3 percent to 20–30 percent. As the success rate improves, scientists expect that many of the clones will be as normal as lambs born by natural means.

·4·
TRANSGENIC CLONES

The term "transgenic" is another way of saying "genetically engineered" that is, resulting from a process that is used to produce hybrid animals containing a gene, the transgene, from a different species. With current technologies, it is possible to produce farm animals, such as sheep, goats, dairy cows, and pigs, that express human genes. Although these animals have only one human gene (among about 20,000 of their own), they are still, technically, animal-human hybrids. The transgene usually codes for a protein that is medically important, such as clotting factors to treat hemophilia. The transgenic animal, always a female, produces the foreign protein in her milk, from which it is easily isolated.

Despite the relatively benign nature of transgenic husbandry, the general public tends to view this kind of research with suspicion and, sometimes, hostility. Cloning mammals for the production of transgenic creatures seems like something that could easily get out of hand. Such worries about dehumanizing scientific experiments have been with us for some time and frequently find expression in literature. H. G. Wells, a famous 19th-century British author, turned the production of human-animal hybrids into a science fiction horror story when he wrote *The Island of Doctor Moreau* (1869). The character Dr. Moreau is obsessed with the idea of producing human-animal hybrids, which he calls the beast-people. On a secluded island, in a laboratory known as the "house of pain," he creates cat-humans, wolf-humans, and other hybrids, all of which are physically monstrous. The beast-people eventually kill Dr. Moreau, leaving the reader with a lesson in morality that may best be summed up in the following way: Don't mess with nature or you will regret it.

H. G. Wells is often given credit for being a visionary, and his book is frequently mentioned in connection with the current production of transgenic animals. But Wells, like his contemporaries, did not foresee the emergence of biotechnology and its ability to mix genes from different species. Dr. Moreau produced his hybrids surgically (or through vivisection, as it was called in Wells's day) by mixing organs and tissues from various animals, all the time blissfully ignorant of the insurmountable problem of cross-species tissue rejection.

Comparing modern transgenic husbandry with the fictional work of Dr. Moreau is a stretch, to say the least, but the emotional force of the book and three subsequent movie versions (*Island of Lost Souls,* 1936, and *The Island of Doctor Moreau,* 1977 and 1996) leaves a powerful impression that is difficult to counter. These ideas came to the movies most recently with the release of *The Lord of the Rings,* by J. R. R. Tolkien, only here it is the evil Sauron who converts the beautiful elves into the loathsome orcs. Tolkien's trilogy was written in the 1930s, and he, like the rest of society, was strongly influenced by the character of Dr. Moreau. These very popular books and movies have influenced people to associate talk of hybrid animals with unpleasant images, but the difference between the beast-people of fiction and the transgenic animals currently being produced is profound. A transgenic sheep or goat looks like any other sheep or goat, and the transgenes they carry, rather than turning them into monsters, will help save the lives of millions of people worldwide.

Designing Biofactories

Transgenic animals are called biofactories because they are able to mass-produce a substance that is harvested and sold, usually as a pharmaceutical product. Although in common usage, it is an unfortunate term in that it gives the impression the animals are treated like inanimate machines. There is, to be sure, an assembly-line quality to a transgenic farm, but no more so than on an ordinary dairy farm or cattle ranch. We have traditionally kept and maintained animals for food and clothing, and now we keep them to produce medicinal drugs.

Transgenic animals are cloned from females. The exceptions to this involve animals that are cloned for organ farming (chapter 5) or for the production of immunoglobulins, which are isolated from the blood. Clones intended to produce medicinal products must be female in order to have the transgene expressed in the mammary gland. If the cloning procedure is successful, the adult clone's body will secrete the protein product into the milk, from which it is easily isolated. The cell-culturing stage of the standard animal-cloning procedure is the stage at which the transgene is added to the cells that serve as nuclear donors (karyoplasts).

The transgene, intended for the production of a useful drug, is always a gene that has been isolated from human cells. For example, sheep have been cloned that produce blood clotting protein IX, for treating hemophiliacs, by introducing the human gene for clotting protein IX into cultured sheep cells. Cells that take up the transgene and incorporate it into their nuclei are used to produce the embryo by the nuclear transfer procedure. (This procedure is described in chapter 2.)

In most cases, the transgene is purchased from a pharmaceutical or biotechnology company that specializes in isolating and characterizing human genes. Characterization of the gene involves obtaining the complete DNA sequence for both the coding and controlling regions of the gene. The coding regions specify the structure of the protein product while the controlling region, known as the promoter, determines when the gene is turned on or off. An important aspect of producing transgenic animals is ensuring the transgene is expressed appropriately. This requires swapping the gene's natural promoter with one that will allow expression of the gene in the target issue.

Swapping promoters can be done using recombinate DNA technology. In the case of human clotting protein IX, its natural promoter ensures that it will be expressed in human bone marrow and nowhere else. If a scientist wishes to have this human gene expressed in the mammary gland of a sheep it is necessary to swap the natural promoter with one that controls the expression of a sheep milk gene. One ingredient of sheep milk is a protein called β-lactoglobulin, a protein that helps stabilize the dominant milk sugar, lactose. Swapping the clotting factor IX gene promoter with an ovine (i.e., sheep) β-lactoglobulin gene promoter will ensure production of the clotting factor in sheep milk.

Drugs from Transgenic Animals

HUMAN CLOTTING FACTOR IX AND HEMOPHILIA

When we cut ourselves, some of our blood, which is normally a liquid, is converted to a fibrous solid at the site of the wound. A blood clot, so formed, has several functions: It reduces blood loss, it covers the wound

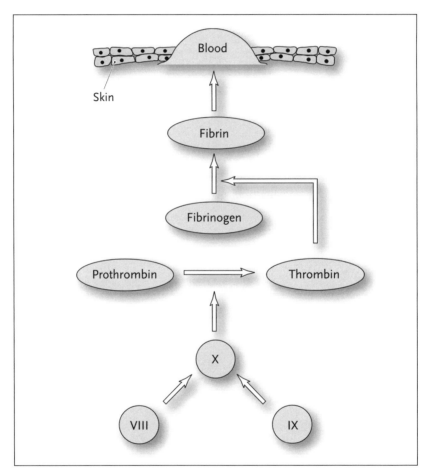

Formation of a blood clot. Two clotting factors (VIII and IX) activate a third (X), which stimulates conversion of prothrombin to thrombin. Thrombin then catalyzes the conversion of fibrinogen to fibrin to convert the drop of blood, collecting at a wound, to a solid clot.

to prevent bacterial infection, and it provides a temporary patch until the cells repair the damage.

The formation of a blood clot is a complex process that involves at least a dozen enzymes and protein factors. The principal elements in the clotting process are the proteins prothrombin, thrombin, and fibrinogen. These proteins are modified in sequence, with the help of several clotting factors, to produce fibrin, the protein from which clots are made.

Hemophilia A is a disease characterized by a failure of the clotting process. It is caused by a mutation in the clotting factor VIII gene (*hema*), located on the X chromosome, affecting 1 in 5,000 males. A second, much rarer form of this disease, identified in 1952, is hemophilia B. This form of the disease is caused by a loss of clotting factor IX. Hemophilia B is sometimes called Christmas disease after Stephen Christmas, the first patient diagnosed with this disease, and, for a time, factor IX was known as the Christmas factor. The chromosomal location of the factor IX gene is unknown. Both clotting factors, VIII and IX, are synthesized in the liver.

A famous carrier of hemophilia A was Queen Victoria, who transmitted it, by the marriages of her children to the royal families of Germany, Spain, and Russia. Males are susceptible to this disease because they have only one X chromosome. Females, with two X chromosomes, are not likely to have a defective *hema* gene on both chromosomes, and hence rarely show the symptoms of this disease.

Conventional treatment of hemophilia A has involved regular transfusions of normal blood to replace the defective clotting factor, but this treatment is a major inconvenience and often leads to liver damage. Contamination of human blood supplies with the AIDS virus, and the resulting infection of many hemophiliacs in the 1980s, forced the development of alternate sources of factor VIII for replacement therapy, including antibody-purified factors and the production of factor VIII using DNA recombinant technology. These procedures produce safe, high-quality clotting factors but are extremely expensive.

Two methods are currently under development to deal with hemophilia: The first is gene therapy, whereby the gene for factor IX is injected into a patient suffering from this disease in the hope that it will provide the normal clotting factor. The second approach involves the production of transgenic cows or sheep that produce clotting factor IX in their milk.

In 1997, the year after Dolly was born, Ian Wilmut's team was successful in producing several transgenic sheep expressing the factor IX gene. Research is now under way to produce factor IX transgenic cows and to assess the safety of this product. Transgenic cows are expected to produce a greater amount of factor IX than sheep do. An individual dairy cow will produce approximately 8,000 liters of milk per year containing an estimated 80 kilograms of factor IX. This is approximately 10 times the expected yield from a sheep. With a worldwide demand for factor IX exceeding half a ton per year, this difference is crucial.

ALPHA-1 ANTITRYPSIN AND CYSTIC FIBROSIS

Of all genetic diseases, cystic fibrosis (CF) is possibly the most debilitating. This disease is associated with the production of thick, sticky mucus that clogs the lungs, making breathing difficult and providing an environment that is susceptible to bacterial infection. Indeed, most sufferers of CF die of congestive lung failure, brought on by a bacterial infection, before the age of 30.

Cystic fibrosis is caused by a mutation in a gene that codes for a sodium chloride transporter, called CFTR, found on the surface of the epithelial cells that line the lungs and other organs. Several hundred mutations have been found in this gene, all of which result in defective transport of sodium and chloride by epithelial cells. The transporter can tolerate some amino acid substitutions, so the severity of the disease varies depending on the site of the mutation. A frequently occurring mutation does not cripple the transporter, but it does alter its three-dimensional shape and, as a consequence, the sorting machinery in the Golgi complex never delivers it to the cell membrane.

The loss of the CF transporter reduces the amount of water on the cell surface, thus increasing the density of the mucus layer, and is responsible for increasing the acidity inside the cell. The abnormal acid level leads to the production of a defective glycocalyx, which is unable to repel bacteria; as a consequence, a specific bacterium, *Pseudomonas aeruginosa*, is free to infect and destroy lung tissue. Conventional treatments are available that thin the mucus layer and kill *Pseudomonas,* but they are only partially successful. Patients suffering from CF must undergo regular treatments to dislodge the mucus in order to clear the airways. For them, life is a daily battle against suffocation.

The battle against cystic fibrosis, like hemophilia, is being fought on two fronts simultaneously: through the development of gene therapy to introduce a normal CFTR gene to the patient's cells, and the production of transgenic cows for the mass production of a protein called alpha-1 antitrypsin. This protein has been used successfully to treat diseases affecting the lungs, such as cystic fibrosis and emphysema.

The air we breathe carries large numbers of bacteria, bacterial spores, dust particles, and pollen. The white blood cells of our immune system deal with these potentially dangerous particles by releasing an enzyme called neutrophil elastase (or simply elastase). This enzyme breaks down foreign particles but can also damage lung tissue if it is not properly regulated. The regulation of elastase is the job of antitrypsin. If too much elastase is released, antitrypsin binds to it, preventing the elastase from damaging lung tissue. Patients suffering from emphysema have an inadequate supply of antitrypsin, so their lungs are damaged by their own immune system, making it difficult for them to breathe. Similarly, children suffering from cystic fibrosis have a chronic lung infection, which stimulates the release of unusually large amounts of elastase. These patients, consequently, need greater than normal amounts of antitrypsin to protect their lungs from damage. The additional antitrypsin must be supplied to these patients in the form of a drug. Current estimates place the worldwide demand for antitrypsin, to fight lung diseases, at just over one ton per year. The synthesis of this protein by transgenic animals is the only way to produce enough of this protein in the quality required for a medicinal drug.

HUMAN ANTIBODIES

In mid-2002 a small biotechnology company in Westport, Connecticut, called Hematech created four transgenic calves that produce human antibodies referred to as immunoglobulin or gamma globulin. Antibodies are proteins that assume a roughly spherical or globular shape (hence the word *globulin*) and are designed by our immune system to attack invading bacteria, protozoans, and viruses.

Immunoglobulin is a mixture of human antibodies given to people with immune system deficiencies or as treatment for infections. It is normally derived from human blood; as a consequence it is usually in short supply. In addition, antibodies for specific diseases can be obtained only from people who acquired the illness through the normal course of their lives. It is both unethical and illegal to expose people to a disease for the express purpose of harvesting antibodies. Transgenic cows, on the other hand, can be exposed to any number of infectious agents, and because of their size, they will produce large quantities of immunoglobulins.

There are no legal restrictions on the use of transgenic animals to produce human antibodies, but whether the procedure is ethical or not is up for debate. The complicating element here is the fact that the cows' own immune system will also produce antibodies, and these would be very difficult to separate from the human antibodies. The solution is to knock out (during the cloning procedure) the cow's immune genes so only the human antibodies would be produced. How this will affect the cows' health is anyone's guess, but in all likelihood they would have to live in a sterile environment: no pastures, no trees, not even a walk through the barnyard. Nevertheless, researchers at Hematech expect to have human antibodies, derived from immune-deficient transgenic cows, ready for market by 2005.

In 2004, a second group of researchers, headed by Dr. Gottfried Brem of the University of Veterinary Medicine in Vienna, Austria, created transgenic rabbits and cattle that produced an antibody, designated r28M, that is able to kill melanoma tumor cells in vitro. Purified from the serum of transgenic animals, the antibody was designated to target glycoproteins in the cell membrane of the tumor cells and to stimulate tumor cell destruction by activating T cells.

HUMAN SERUM ALBUMIN (HSA)

HSA is a major component of blood plasma and is involved in maintaining the balance of fluids between the blood and the tissues. It also regulates the transport of amino acids, fatty acids, hormones, drugs, and drug metabolites. Clinical uses include fluid volume replacement for patients suffering from shock and serious burns, fluid administration during surgery, and for AIDS and cancer therapies. HSA is also an important stabilizer that is added to antisera, such as polio, cholera, and smallpox vaccines. HSA is, in itself, a powerful incentive for obtaining human proteins from transgenic animals. Worldwide demand for HSA exceeds 600 tons per year, with sales of nearly $1.3 billion.

Transgenic cows are the only means by which the enormous world-wide demand for HSA can be met. However, cow's milk contains an albumin that is very difficult to separate from its human counterpart. Consequently, researchers are trying to produce knockout transgenic cows that express HSA but lack the gene for their milk albumin. This problem is similar to that already described for obtaining human anti-bodies from transgenic cows, but in the case of HSA, the knockout cows would retain a functional immune system and thus could be raised as ordinary dairy cows.

Spider Silk from Goats

Drugs are not the only products obtained from transgenic animals. Nexia Biotechnologies, located on a former maple-sugar farm in rural Quebec, has produced transgenic goats that express the gene for spider's silk. As with the other transgenic products described, the silk gene is expressed only in the mammary gland, so the silk protein is released in the milk, from which it is isolated. Spider's silk is an extremely tough material that has five times the strength of steel and, according to Nexia's president and C.E.O., Dr. Jeffrey Turner, can be used to make fishing line and nets, biodegradable surgical sutures, ultra-light garments and sewing thread, tennis racket strings, body armor, and many other things.

Nexia's body armor has attracted the attention of the Pentagon, and with its financial backing, the company has set up a second plant in New York that will produce spider's silk under the trademark name of BioSteel. A bulletproof vest made from BioSteel would be just a bit thicker than nylon and practically weightless. Such a material was anticipated by Tolkien when he wrote *The Lord of the Rings:* "As tough as dragon scales and light as a feather," said Bilbo Baggins to his nephew Frodo, upon presenting him with a protective vest of near-magical properties made by the dwarves from a mysterious material called mithril. The convergence of fantasy and science reality appears to be in the making.

·5·
ORGAN FARMING

Organ transplantation, involving the heart, lungs, liver, pancreas, and kidneys, is a powerful medical procedure that saves thousands of lives every year. The success of this procedure, however, has led to a great disparity between the number of people needing a transplant and the number of donated organs that are available. In 2003 more than 80,000 people were on a waiting list for an organ transplant in the United States alone; of these, only 24,861 received an organ, while more than 6,000 patients died because an organ could not be found for them. Despite a concerted effort on the part of the medical community to encourage organ donation, the number of people willing to do so has not changed since the 1990s.

In an effort to offset the grossly inadequate supply of organs, many scientists have studied the possibility of using organs obtained from pigs, which have hearts, kidneys, lungs, and pancreata very similar to those found in humans. Theoretically, pigs could be a ready source of these organs, thus making up the difference between patient need and donor availability. If such a plan worked, human organ donation could become obsolete.

However, the human immune system, designed to seek out and destroy foreign cells, has created a tremendous obstacle to the success of human-to-human (i.e., allogeneic) transplants and has so far rendered pig-to-human (i.e., xenogeneic) transplants a therapy of the distant future. Nevertheless, medical researchers agree that the future of organ transplants lies with xenotransplantation. Conventional allogeneic organ transplants, while only partially successful, are providing valuable information regarding tissue rejection and the many things that must be done to ensure a happy union between the transplant and the patient's immune system.

Conventional Organ Transplants

The kidney was the first organ to be transplanted, in the 1950s, and in 1967 the South African surgeon Dr. Christiaan Barnard performed the first successful heart transplant. This accomplishment was quickly followed by several other heart transplantations at Stanford University, in the United States. But the initial enthusiasm for kidney and heart transplantation was stifled by the sudden deaths of all the first transplant patients, due to immune rejection of the grafted organs. During the 1970s, an immunosuppressant drug called azothioprine was introduced, which improved the survival of transplant patients, but rejection was still a major problem, with fewer than 40 percent of the patients surviving for one year after surgery. In 1983 a second, more powerful immunosuppressant, called cyclosporine, was introduced. This drug increased the one-year survival rate for kidney and heart transplant patients to more than 80 percent, opening the door to the successful transplantation of other organs, such as lungs, liver, and pancreata. Since the introduction of cyclosporine, additional immunosuppressants have been discovered, the most important of which are prednisone and tacrolimus. (We will return to the role these drugs play in organ transplantation in a later section.)

KIDNEY TRANSPLANTATION

The kidney is the organ most commonly transplanted; failure of the patient's original kidney is usually due to damage brought on by diabetes. In 1992, in the United States alone, 9,671 people received a donor kidney, increasing to 15,120 just 10 years later (see table on page 50). The lack of donated kidneys to meet the demand for kidney transplants has worsened over the years. In 1992 the number of Americans on the waiting list for a kidney transplant was 22,063, increasing to an astonishing 58,432 patients by 2002, nearly four times the number of available organs. The short-term success of kidney transplantation is impressive, with 95.8 percent of the transplant patients surviving the first year, but survival drops to 69.4 percent by the 10-year mark (see table on page 51).

Survival of the patient, particularly for a kidney transplant, is usually better than the survival of the grafted organ. Survival of the grafted kidney, at the one-year mark, is 91.4 percent, but organ survival drops sharply to 45.9 percent by the 10-year mark, considerably lower than the survival rate of the patients (see table on page 51). The difference in survivability between the patient and the grafted kidney is due to the fact that when the organ fails, the patient may receive a second kidney transplant if a donor organ is available, or the patient may be kept alive with kidney dialysis. Thus it is the survival of the grafted organ that gives the truest picture of the overall success of organ transplantation. The heart, for obvious reasons, is the only case where survival of the graft and the patient correspond.

CARDIAC TRANSPLANTATION

Heart transplants are usually performed on patients who have sustained severe damage to their cardiomyocytes (heart muscle) because of blocked or clogged carotid arteries (the arteries that supply the heart with blood). These patients are generally middle-aged (50 to 60 years old), but there are also many infants and children who require a heart

THE NUMBER OF ORGAN TRANSPLANTS AND WAIT-LISTED PATIENTS IN THE UNITED STATES

	1992		2002	
	Transplants	Wait-listed	Transplants	Wait-listed
Kidney	9,729	22,063	15,120	58,432
Heart	2,171	2,655	2,057	3,503
Liver	3,036	5,789	5,671	17,460
Lung	535	1,258	1,085	3,931
Pancreas	64	139	502	1,610
Total	15,535	31,904	24,435	84,936

Source: United Network for Organ Sharing. Data is shown for single-organ transplants, but some patients require two organs, which are transplanted at the same time. Heart-lung and kidney-pancreas transplants are the most common examples. Multiorgan transplants, as well as those involving the intestine, brought the number of wait-listed patients in 2003 to 85,351.

SURVIVAL OF TRANSPLANT PATIENTS AND TRANSPLANTED ORGANS IN THE UNITED STATES

	1 year		5 year		10 year	
	Patients	Organs	Patients	Organs	Patients	Organs
Kidney	95.8	91.4	84.8	69.9	69.4	45.9
Heart	85.1	84.4	69.8	68.1	50.0	46.4
Liver	85.8	78.2	79.0	68.2	72.3	43.9
Lung	77.4	87.3	42.5	40.5	22.7	17.5
Pancreas	98.6	81.2	77.8	32.4	68.2	16.2

Table values are percentages. The data was compiled from information provided by the United Network for Organ Sharing for 2002.

transplant due to congenital defects in the cardiomyocytes or gross anatomy of the heart or the heart valves.

Since the immunosuppressant cyclosporine was introduced in the 1980s, the number of heart transplants in the United States has increased from about a dozen in the late 1970s to 2,171 in 1992, an annual rate that remained relatively constant through 2003. As with the kidney, the number of heart transplants is limited by donor supply, since more than 3,000 patients were on the waiting list in 2003 (see table on page 50). The number of heart transplants is also limited by the high cost of the procedure, currently estimated to be $200,000 (U.S.) for the first year. In addition, there is a $10,000 to $30,000 yearly cost for immunosuppressant drugs and follow-up procedures. These costs are particularly hard to meet in countries without medical insurance. The current one- and five-year patient survival rates are 85 and 70 percent. However, only 46 percent of the grafted hearts (and 50 percent of the patients) survive to the 10-year mark (see table above).

The dismal 10-year survival rate is due primarily to chronic rejection of the heart by the immune system. The daily diet of immunosuppressant drugs, prescribed for all transplant patients, inhibits the immune response but does not abolish it completely. Day by day, the immune system launches small attacks on the foreign tissue, causing damage at the cellular level that over time leads to failure of the entire organ. Fifty percent of heart transplant patients show clear signs of this progression before the five-year mark.

When the transplanted heart is finally rejected, the patient's physician may recommend a second transplant, if an organ is available, but the one-year survival rate for a second transplant is very poor. Compounding the problem is the patient's poor health, brought on not only by a failing heart but also by the immunosuppressants, which make it difficult for the patient to fend off several forms of cancer, in addition to a large number of infectious diseases.

LIVER TRANSPLANTATION

The biochemistry and physiology of the liver are extremely complex. This organ is charged with several important tasks: the removal of potentially toxic compounds from the blood; the production of substances, called bile salts, that are secreted into the intestine where they are involved in the digestion of fatty compounds; and the storage of amino acids and glucose (as glycogen). Detoxification of the blood is primarily concerned with the conversion of ammonia, which is lethal at high concentrations, to urea, a compound that is safely excreted by the kidneys. This process is carried out by a series of enzymes known as the urea cycle. Failure of this cycle is a common liver disorder that is often treated with transplant surgery. Other liver diseases that are treated with a transplant are chronic hepatitis, cirrhosis, and cancer. Many cases of liver cirrhosis are preventable, as they are brought on by excessive consumption of alcohol. There are also many inherited disorders of liver metabolism, that primarily affect children, such as hemophilia and glycogen storage diseases, which are treated with whole or partial liver transplants.

Liver transplantation was pioneered in the 1960s at the University of Pittsburgh and in Cambridge, England. The procedure is now performed routinely in many medical centers throughout North America and Western Europe. In 1992 there were 3,036 liver transplants performed in the United States, with 5,789 patients on the waiting list. The number of liver transplants nearly doubled by 2003, while those on the waiting list increased to more than 17,000 (see table on page 50). The one-year patient survival is better than 85 percent, although organ survival drops dramatically, to 44 percent, by the 10-year mark.

LUNG TRANSPLANTATION

Emphysema, a lung disorder frequently brought on by cigarette smoke, accounts for almost 60 percent of all lung transplants, with cystic fibrosis accounting for the remainder (these diseases were described in chapter 4). Transplantation of the lung was first attempted in 1980, but the surgical procedures were not perfected until 1989, after which the number of transplants increased dramatically. Worldwide, the International Society for Heart and Lung Transplantation reported 900 lung transplants involving one or both lungs in 1994, followed by a dramatic increase to 8,997 transplants in 1999. In the United States, 535 lung transplants were performed in 1992, increasing to more than 1,000 by 2003. As with other organ transplants, the ratio of wait-listed patients to transplants performed has increased remarkably since the 1990s. In 1992 the number of patients waiting for a lung transplant was about double the number of transplants performed, but by 2003, wait-listed patients outnumbered transplants by four to one (see table on page 50). The one-year survival rate for lung transplant patients is 77 percent: Survival drops to 23 percent at the 10-year mark (see table on page 51).

Diseases affecting the lungs, such as emphysema, often affect the heart as well. Damaged lungs are incapable of supplying enough oxygen to keep the cardiomyocytes healthy. It is for this reason that patients suffering from lung diseases often require simultaneous heart-lung transplants; 29 such procedures were carried out in 2003. The heart-lung transplant survival rate is poor: 56 percent at one year and less than 20 percent at 10 years.

PANCREAS TRANSPLANTATION

Failure of the pancreas is associated with the onset of type I diabetes. This disease is characterized by a failure of special cells in the pancreas, called beta cells, that produce insulin, a hormone that regulates the uptake of glucose by virtually every cell in the body. Diabetes often damages the kidneys, and for this reason, transplantation of the pancreas often follows, or is performed simultaneously with, a kidney transplant.

Despite the link between kidney and pancreas failure, transplantation of the pancreas is rare, with only 64 cases reported in 1992, and 502 in 2003 (see table on page 50). This is because pancreatic failure can be treated for many years with insulin injections. Pancreas transplant patients show a one-year survival rate of more than 98 percent, but the survival of the organ after five years is only 32 percent, and it drops at the 10-year mark to 16 percent.

ORGAN PROCUREMENT

Obtaining organs for the many thousands of patients needing a transplant each year requires the coordinated effort of a virtual army of health professionals. In the United States, there are six principal organizations involved in organ procurement (see table below).

Donor organs are obtained by 59 Organ Procurement Organizations (OPOs), which provide organs to 287 organ transplant centers. The OPOs are under the direction of governmental agencies, such as the Centers for Medicare and Medicaid Services (CMS) and the Health Resources and Services Administration (HRSA). The HRSA also funds the Scientific Registry of Transplant Recipients (SRTR), which maintains an organ transplant database and information center. Every OPO is a member of the Organ Procurement and Transplantation Network (OPTN), which is maintained by the United Network for Organ Sharing (UNOS). The rules for organ allocation, set by OPTN and UNOS, are computerized to enhance the speed, efficiency, and fairness of matching a donor organ with one of the 85,351 patients currently registered with OPTN. The fairness of the distribution rules is especially important given the chronic shortage of organs. As already mentioned, several thousand people die every year in the United States while waiting for an organ. Thus the

ORGAN TRANSPLANT ORGANIZATIONS IN THE UNITED STATES	
Name	**Abbreviation**
Organ Procurement Organization	OPO
Centers for Medicare and Medicaid Services	CMS
Organ Procurement and Transplantation Network	OPTN
United Network for Organ Sharing	UNOS
Health Resources and Services Administration	HRSA
Scientific Registry of Transplant Recipients	SRTR

decisions made by OPTN and UNOS regarding who gets an organ and who does not mean life for some but death for many others.

Matching Tissues

A molecular forest, called the glycocalyx, covers the surface of every cell and has a central role in the process of matching tissues for transplant operations. The trees in the cell's forest are glycoproteins

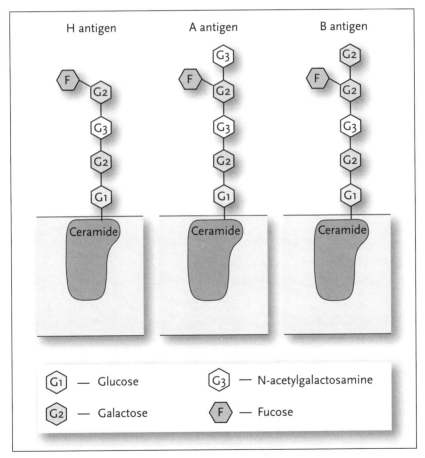

The ABO antigens on the surface of red blood cells. All individuals have the H antigen. In addition, 41 percent of North Americans have the A antigen, 10 percent have B, 4 percent have both A and B, and 45 percent have neither. The last group is said to be type O.

and glycolipids that have "trunks" made of protein or lipid and "leaves" made of sugar. These molecular trees are embedded in the cell membrane, much like the trees of Earth are rooted in the soil.

The exact composition of the glycocalyx varies with each individual, just as an Earth forest located at the equator is different from one located in the Northern Hemisphere. The human immune system uses the spatial arrangement of the exposed sugar groups to decide whether a cell is foreign or not. Thus the glycocalyx is like a cell's fingerprint, and if that fingerprint does not pass the recognition test, the cell is destroyed or is forced to commit suicide. Immunologists refer to the glycoproteins and glycolipids in the glycocalyx as cell-surface antigens. The term antigen arises from the fact that cell-surface glycoproteins on a foreign cell can generate a response from the immune system that leads to the production of antibodies capable of binding to and destroying the foreign cell.

An extremely important pair of cell-surface glycolipids are known as the A and B antigens. These glycolipids occur on the surface of red blood cells and form the ABO blood group system that determines each individual's basic blood type. The A and B antigens are derived from a third antigen, called H, which all individuals possess. Blood type A is produced by the *A* gene, which codes for a glycosyl transferase that adds an N-acetylgalactosamine to the H antigen. Blood type B is produced by a different transferase that places a galactose molecule on the H antigen. Some individuals have both A and B transferases and thus are said to have blood type AB. Individuals with blood type O have neither transferase. In North America, blood types A and O dominate, with A occurring in 41 percent of the population and O in 45 percent. Blood types B and AB are rare, with B occurring at a frequency of 10 percent and AB at only 4 percent.

An individual who is blood type A forms antibodies against the B antigen and therefore cannot receive blood from a type B individual, but he or she can receive blood from type O individuals. Similarly, a type B individual cannot receive blood from someone with blood type A but can receive it from someone who is type O. Individuals who have blood type AB can receive blood from individuals who have blood types A, B, or O, and therefore such individuals are called universal recipients. On the other hand, people with blood type O can receive only type O blood because they will form antibodies against both A and B antigens. While individuals with type AB blood are universal recipients, individuals with type O blood are called universal donors because their blood may be given to anyone without fear of invoking an immune response.

The importance of blood type with respect to organ transplantation is best illustrated by the recent case of Jesica Santillan, a 17-year-old girl who required a heart-lung transplant to correct a congenital lung defect that also damaged her heart. On February 7, 2003, physicians at Duke University Hospital in Durham, North Carolina, replaced Jesica's heart and lungs without checking the blood type of the donor. Jesica was blood type O, but the donor was type A. Jesica's immune system rejected the mismatched organs, and she lapsed into a deep coma soon after the operation was completed. In a desperate attempt to correct the mistake, Jesica's surgeons replaced the mismatched heart and lungs with organs obtained from a type O donor, but it was too late. Jesica had already suffered severe and irreparable brain damage, and on February 22, 2003, she died.

As critically important as they are to the success of transplant surgery, the A and B antigens are only two of many thousands of cell-surface antigens that play a role in the rejection of foreign tissue. A second major group of antigens, called the human leukocyte antigens (HLA), may in fact number in the millions. These antigens are glycoproteins that cover the surface of virtually every cell in the body, not just leukocytes (they are called leukocyte antigens simply because that was the cell from which they were originally identified). When faced with this level of complexity, transplant surgeons have had to content themselves with matching only five or six of the most common HLA antigens between the recipient and donor. This, of course, leaves many mismatched antigens, but it seems that some antigens elicit a much stronger immune response than others, an effect that is likely quantitative in nature. That is, a million copies of antigen X will catch the attention of the immune system much more effectively than would 10 copies of antigen Y. By matching the dominant antigens, surgeons hope to avoid what is called the hyper-acute immune response, which leads to the immediate destruction of the transplanted organ and death of the patient. It was a hyper-acute response, brought on by a mismatch of dominant antigens, that killed Jesica Santillan. Matching dominant antigens does not mean the transplanted organ is compatible, only that the patient has a good chance of surviving the first year. Beyond that, the immune system begins a slow chronic attack on the remaining mismatched antigens, leading to eventual failure of most transplanted organs. The slow chronic attack is responsible for the poor five- and 10-year survival of transplant patients previously cited.

The Human Immune System

All immune systems are designed to protect an individual from invading microbes, particularly bacteria and viruses. Such a system does not understand the difference between a bacterium and a cell associated with a transplanted organ; as far as the immune system is concerned, both are foreign and need to be destroyed. Full success with organ and tissue transplants may be possible someday, but it will take a thorough understanding of our immune system and the methods it uses to fight invading cells. Equipped with that knowledge we may be able to retrain the immune system to accept transplanted organs—or at least to find a way to shield those organs from attack—to prevent their ultimate destruction.

The human immune system is composed of a large group of white blood cells that are divided into three major categories: granulocytes, monocytes, and lymphocytes. Granulocytes have a distinctive, lobular nucleus, and all are phagocytic. Monocytes are large phagocytic cells, with an irregularly shaped nucleus. The largest monocytes, the macrophages, can engulf whole bacteria as well as damaged or senescent body cells. Lymphocytes have a smooth morphology and a large round nucleus. T-lymphocytes and natural killer (NK) cells deal primarily with coordinating the immune response and with killing already infected body cells. B-lymphocytes are nonphagocytic; they deal with an invading microbe by releasing antibodies.

Phagocytosis of an invading microbe by granulocytes and monocytes represents a first-line defense, called the innate response. All animals are capable of mounting this kind of defense. Activation of the lymphocytes leads to a more powerful, second line of defense, called the adaptive response, which is found only in higher vertebrates and is initiated by monocytes, specifically, dendritic and Langerhans cells. These cells, after

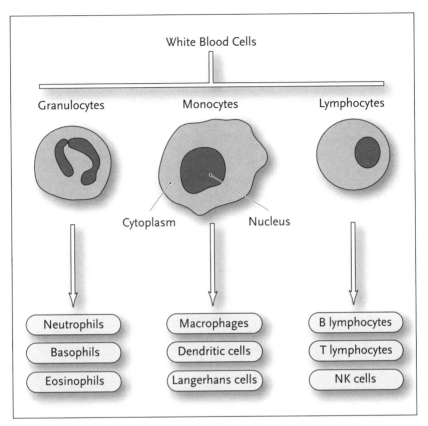

White blood cells. These cells are divided into three major categories: granulocytes, monocytes, and lymphocytes. Granulocytes have a distinctive, lobular nucleus and are phagocytic (eat cells, viruses, and debris). Monocytes are large cells with an irregularly shaped nucleus. All monocytes are phagocytic; the largest members, the macrophages, can engulf whole bacteria and damaged or senescent body cells. Lymphocytes have a smooth morphology with a large round nucleus. B-lymphocytes are nonphagocytic but produce antibodies. T-lymphocytes and natural killer (NK) cells coordinate the immune response and can force infected cells to commit suicide.

engulfing a virus or bacteria, literally tear the microbe apart and then embed the pieces, now called antigens, in their membrane. The antigens are presented to lymphocytes, which become activated when their receptors bind to the microbial antigens. Activated B-lymphocytes secrete antibodies specifically designed for that particular microbe. Activated

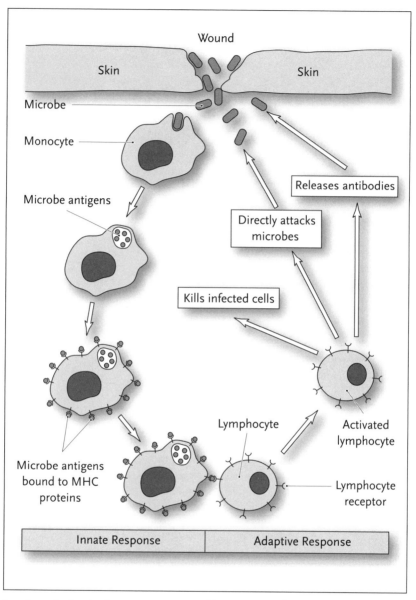

Innate and adaptive immune response. Phagocytosis of invading microbes is called the innate response. In higher vertebrates, microbe antigens, bound to special monocyte surface proteins called the major histocompatibility complex (MHC), are then presented to lymphocytes. Contact between the lymphocyte receptor and the antigen activates the lymphocyte and the adaptive response, consisting of a three-pronged attack on the microbe and microbe-infected cells.

T-cells and NK cells attack the microbe directly but are primarily concerned with locating and killing infected body cells.

The T-cell receptor is aided in the process of activation by a large number of coreceptors, called CD1 through CD120. CD4 ad CD8 are commonly involved in mediating the activation of T-cells by mono-cytes. The abbreviation "CD" stands for cluster of differentiation, meaning the coreceptor aids in the differentiation of the T cells. These coreceptors were originally identified by different groups of researchers using several hundred different antibodies. Eventually, they realized that many of the antibodies, referred to now as a cluster, were identifying the same coreceptor. Once activated, T-cells recruit other T-cells by secreting special, lymphocyte-specific growth factors called inter-leukins. More than 30 different interleukins have been identified, and they are referred to as IL-1 through IL-30.

The adaptive system can remember a pathogen long after it has been removed from the body. This why a specific bacteria or virus cannot make us sick twice. Once infected, we develop a natural, lifelong immunity. We can also immunize ourselves against many diseases by injecting a crippled version of the pathogen, or specific antigens from a pathogen, into our bloodstream. This concoction of bits and pieces from a pathogen, called an immunizing serum, activates the adaptive response, leading to a lasting, though not always lifelong, immunity against the disease. It is the adaptive system that is responsible for the rejection of a transplanted organ; immunosupressants, given to all transplant patients, are effective because they cripple this part of the human immune system.

Suppressing the Immune System

Blocking the immune response after transplant surgery is important, even in those cases where the major antigens have been matched. Prior to effective immunosuppressive therapy, transplant patients were lucky to survive the first few weeks following surgery. The current therapy is based on a collection of drugs and hormones that partially block the adaptive response, leaving the innate response largely intact. Immunosuppressants currently in use are azathioprine, cyclosporine, tacrolimus, glucocorticoids, and antibodies.

AZATHIOPRINE

This drug was first used in the 1970s to improve the one-year survival of heart and kidney transplant patients, and is a molecule closely related to purines (important components of DNA and RNA nucleotides). Because of its similarity to purines, azathioprine can block both DNA and RNA synthesis. Activation of the adaptive immune response depends on the reproduction, through mitosis, of white blood cells; therefore, azathioprine is an effective immunosuppressant. Many patients, however, are especially sensitive to this drug and often develop serious side effects, leading to damaged kidneys, jaundice, and anemia.

CYCLOSPORINE

This compound is a fungal peptide that specifically blocks transcription of mRNA for many of the interleukins, thereby inhibiting T-cell proliferation. The main side effect with this drug, as with azathioprine, is nephrotoxicity (i.e., damage to the nephron, the blood-filtering component of the kidney). In the case of a kidney transplant, it is often difficult to distinguish a rejection episode from cyclosporine-induced damage.

TACROLIMUS

This is a fungal compound that has the same mode of action as cyclosporine, but the side effects are not as severe. However, while this drug has a lower nephrotoxicity than cyclosporine, it has a greater tendency to induce diabetes mellitus. Because diabetes is more easily treated than kidney damage, this drug is regarded as less toxic overall and is beginning to replace cyclosporine.

GLUCOCORTICOIDS

A class of steroid hormones produced by the adrenal cortex called glucocorticoids have been used as effective immunosupressants. A synthetic glucocorticoid called prednisone blocks the release of the interleukins IL-1 and IL-6, thus interfering with the activation of the adaptive immune response. This hormone is most effective when used in conjunction with either cyclosporine or tacrolimus. Extensive use of prednisone has severe side effects, most notably impairment of wound healing (including surgical incisions) and heightened predisposition to infection. Success with this hormone has been achieved with an alternate-day course of treatment.

ANTIBODIES

Research is currently underway to produce antibodies that bind to and inactivate the CD coreceptors located on T-cells. Different subpopulations of T-cells express different CD molecules. Consequently, the use of tailor-made antibodies could provide a highly specific method for suppressing only a portion of the immune response, thus minimizing serious side effects.

Artificial Organs

Artificial hearts and kidneys have been available since the 1970s and have been useful in maintaining seriously ill patients while they wait for a transplant or for new medical procedures that might restore their organs to health. Artificial kidneys have changed little over the years, but artificial hearts have improved considerably.

Artificial kidneys are called dialysis machines and are about the size of a small student's desk. The patient's circulation is diverted through the machine by two catheters, one carrying blood to the machine from an artery, and a second that returns the purified blood to the patient through a vein in the leg. Patients with severe kidney damage can expect to be connected to a dialysis machine for an hour or more, several days a week.

The first artificial hearts were also large external machines that the patient was connected to. In the 1980s an American physician named Robert Jarvik introduced the first implantable artificial heart, the Jarvik-1, a device about the size of a real heart. In 1982, a team led by William DeVries of the University of Utah implanted an improved model, the Jarvik-7, into a patient named Barney Clark, who was not eligible for a transplant and was not expected to live for more than 30 days. Although the Jarvik-7 was small enough to be implanted, its power source was a large external air compressor that was a great hindrance to the patient's mobility. A second, and even more serious, disadvantage of the Jarvik-7 was the excessive turbulence it generated, which led to the formation of many blood clots. Blood clots are extremely dangerous because they can plug fine capillaries in the brain, causing a stroke, and they can plug the fine tubules in the kidney (the nephrons), leading to severe kidney damage and, ultimately, multiorgan failure. Barney Clark died from a severe stroke and kidney damage 112 days after receiving the Jarvik-7.

Abiomed Incorporated, a company that has been developing biomedical equipment for many years, introduced a much-improved implantable mechanical heart in 2000. Their mechanical heart, called the AbioCor, has two main advantages over the Jarvik-7. First, it does not require a bulky external power source but instead is run by a small battery pack that the patient wears on a belt around the waist. Second, the design includes a smooth flow chamber to reduce turbulence and the occurrence of blood clots. The American Food and Drug Administration (FDA) approved the AbioCor for clinical trials on January 30, 2001, and by February 2003, physicians at the University of Louisville's Health Science Center, in Danvers, Massachusetts, had fitted eight patients with one of these hearts. The maximum survival time of nearly two years attained by one of the patients was a dramatic improvement over the record of the Jarvik-7. However, for the remaining patients, survival was still measured in days (from 54 to 150 days), not years.

Mechanical hearts have come a long way in 30 years, and even greater improvements may be possible in the coming years. But for the time being, these devices are still very much in the developmental stage, and they cannot compete with the results obtained for transplants of real hearts.

The Future of Organ Transplants

A mechanical heart, no matter how well designed, is no match for the real thing. But real hearts, donated for transplant surgery, are in short supply. A seemingly ideal solution to this problem is to use hearts from farm animals, particularly from pigs, because they have human-sized organs. The catch to all of this, of course, is the human immune system: Without being suppressed, it does not allow an allograft (human organ transplant), and if confronted with a xenograft (animal organ transplant), the immune systems launches an all-out attack on the grafted tissue, known as a hyperacute response. Retraining the immune system to accept a xenograft is for the time being out of the question. But it may be possible to genetically engineer donor pigs so they lack the glycosyltransferases that produce the cell-surface antigens. An alternative is to produce transgenic pigs that express human cell-surface antigens. This is equivalent to producing a humanlike glycocalyx on the surface of pig cells. In either case, the human immune system would treat the pig's heart as though it were an allograft, not a xenograft. The organ would still be attacked, as any nonrelated, human-to-human transplant would be, but the attack is controllable with immunosuppressive therapy. This would solve the organ supply problem, and the patient's outlook for long-term survival would be much better than it would be with a mechanical heart.

To this end, researchers in the United States, Europe, and Japan have cloned transgenic pigs expressing human cell surface antigens, as well as "knockout pigs" that lack the gene for α-1-galactosyltransferase. These animals improve the success of xenotransplantation, but many tests must be performed before clinical trials can begin. Perhaps by 2005, xenotransplants will become a practical reality.

.6.

ETHICS OF ANIMAL CLONING

Until recently, the idea of animal cloning wafted around a few research laboratories as an abstract concept that was fun ͺo ponder but not to be taken seriously. Dolly changed all that. Since the day she was born, scientists, politicians, philosophers, and the general public have been debating the ethical consequences of animal cloning. Dolly converted what was once an idle topic of conversation into something that could affect us all, a new technology that could rejuvenate our medical science and revolutionize animal husbandry.

Scientists like to think they have a solid grip on this technology and are comfortable with its future prospects. But when something looks too good to be true, it is wise to step back and ask the simple question: What will it cost us? Not in dollars and cents, but in the ideas and beliefs we have about our culture and ourselves—ideas and beliefs that have taken thousands of years to develop and now stand at the core of our legal and moral systems. Yes, animal cloning will revolutionize animal husbandry, but it will also change forever the way we think about our families, our children, and ourselves.

These assessments may seem overstated; after all, identical twins are clones of each other, and there seems to be no great problem there. But twinning is a natural event and, more important, one that brings life, not one that takes life away. Animal cloning, on the other hand, has become linked with human abortion, a potentially explosive association. Before dealing with the ethical consequences of this association, however, let us examine the array of ethical problems associated with only the cloning of farm and research animals.

Farm Animals

Animal rights groups have long complained about the living conditions of farm animals, many of which are confined in cramped quarters without enough room for proper exercise, let alone a normal quality of life. Although there are humane societies that protect them from outright cruelty and abuse, farm animals have no legal rights. These animals have been domesticated and are kept on farms to provide us with food, drink, and clothing, and as long as they are treated fairly, society seems to be happy with the arrangement.

Given this situation, what could cloning do to make these animals worse off than they already are? The ethical dilemma of cloning farm animals falls under the category of cruelty and abuse. This is not to say that cloning a farm animal is cruel and abusive but simply that the potential is there. The current efficiency of animal cloning is extremely low. This means that in addition to many stillbirths and naturally aborted fetuses, there are many live births of abnormal offspring that will be afflicted with a higher proportion of diseases and disabilities than would a naturally conceived animal. Given that we know the risks—having seen, for example, cloned animals struggle because of an early onset of arthritis or lung disease brought on by a defective immune system— is it right to go on cloning these creatures? Scientists answer this question with a qualified no: No, it is not right to clone animals if they will suffer unduly, but if the cloning-related disease is mild or controllable, then for the sake of discovery, the experiments should continue.

Moreover, what we see as an unethical procedure now may only be an artifact of cloning's current state of development. Perhaps 10 years from now, after the technology improves, cloned animals will be as healthy as naturally conceived animals, and therefore the ethical dilemma will disappear. They will become, in effect, just other farm animals, no better off, but no worse off, either.

Research Animals

The overall dilemma of cloning research animals is very similar to that described for farm animals. But research animals deserve a separate discussion because there are some important differences. Farm animals are kept for food, while research animals are kept to further our knowledge of biology, most of which is used to develop new medical technologies that often save many thousands of lives.

The question of cruelty and abuse still exists, but now the ethical issues are more complex. Is it wrong to clone a research animal that may suffer physically as a consequence of being cloned if that suffering will, somewhere down the road, relieve the suffering of thousands, possibly millions, of people? The answer among the research community is, again, a qualified no: No, it is not wrong, but it depends on the extent of the suffering and the type of research animal that is being used. Biology departments in North America and Western Europe have set up special committees that monitor the use of research animals and try to ensure that their treatment is humane. Researchers must inform these committees of their intent and justify the use of an animal, particularly if the animal will suffer as a consequence of the research. The committee members must then decide whether the merits of the experiment justify the expected suffering of the animal. Many researchers use mice, rats, rabbits, dogs, and cats. The decision to allow an invasive experiment on any of these animals is fairly straightforward, and invasive experiments are rarely rejected. Hundreds of cancer research centers routinely subject these animals to very uncomfortable experiments in which the animals are given a severe case of skin or organ cancer. Compared with these experiments, the side effects of cloning are mild.

The decision to allow an experiment to proceed becomes much more difficult when animals closely related to humans, such as baboons and chimpanzees, are used. No one would subject these animals to the kinds of experiments that rats and mice routinely undergo. This difference is even more striking if we compare experiments on insects with those performed on vertebrate species. There are no guidelines for insects. Researchers using locusts, houseflies, cockroaches, and any number of other insect species may do what they like with them. A famous English insect physiologist, Vincent B. Wigglesworth, made stunning discoveries by cutting the abdomen off one bug and attaching it with bee's wax to the abdomen of another insect. Many studies involving insect endocrinology entail cutting the head off an adult locust, sealing the wound with wax, and then, by injecting nutrients into the abdomen, keeping the animal alive in that state for several weeks.

The ethical dilemma of animal experimentation increases in severity and complexity as we move up the evolutionary ladder. We, of course, feel more empathy for mammals, and we are especially protective of those mammals close to us—our pets, our farm animals, and especially our closest relatives, the primates. Society will allow scientists to experiment on these animals, but it had better be an important experiment, and it should not cause extreme suffering. The natural extension of this ethical system is our abhorrence of experimenting on human beings. But society does condone human experimentation as long as it is done according to certain accepted guidelines. Experiments using human subjects are called clinical trials, and they form an essential part of modern-day medical research. Indeed, medical procedures are not approved for general use until they are tested in one or more clinical trials. We, as a society, accept clinical trials because they are conducted with the fully informed consent of the human experimental subjects. We will see in the next section how the concept of informed consent has led to a heated debate when it comes to the idea of cloning humans.

Human Beings

Practically from the day that Dolly was born, speculation about the cloning of humans began to grow. The initial enthusiasm for cloning humans may have been caused by the sheer novelty of the idea, since there were few in the scientific community or the general public who could offer sound reasons for attempting such a thing. Vague notions about immortality and the ability to replace extra-bright people gave way to more practical motivations, such as replacing a loved one or making it possible for sterile or same-sex couples to have children.

Scientists involved in the cloning of Dolly and, in particular, Ian Wilmut, the team leader, made it clear very early on that cloning is not an avenue to immortality. A person's clone would be an identical twin, not a replacement. The two would look alike, talk alike, and maybe even dress alike. But they would be distinct individuals, with their own memories and separate identities. The idea of using cloning to replace gifted individuals naturally raises the question of just what constitutes a gifted individual and who will get to decide what those characteristics are. Is winning a prize, such as a Noble Prize, a reliable benchmark for cloning eligibility? People who work in blue-collar jobs, or perhaps do not work at all, are just as likely to have the human qualities that we should all strive for. This is a profound ethical dilemma. It presupposes that humans have the wisdom to know what kind of person will improve our societies and make the world a better place for us all. Yet who can claim such wisdom? And therefore, who can claim that cloning, for the purpose of enhancing the human race, is a good idea?

If it is unwise to clone people to improve the human race, does it follow that it is also unwise to allow sterile or same-sex couples to use cloning so they can have children? Theoretically, there is nothing wrong with couples wanting to clone themselves as a way to start a family; various invertebrate species have been doing so, with great success, for a very long time. However, at the present time, it is an unethical choice to make. Cloning, as made clear by the Dolly experiment, is very inefficient. Most animal clone embryos die before reaching full term, while many others die in the course of being born. Those clones that make it to adulthood are likely to carry subtle genetic abnormalities that weaken their immune system and make them susceptible to obesity and arthritis. Do we want to subject human children to these conditions? Probably not, given that sterile couples today have the option of starting a family by using standard in vitro fertilization techniques or by adopting a child.

As an ethical dilemma, cloning for reproduction is a difficult, but not insurmountable, problem. Ethical objections, particularly concerning therapeutic cloning, fall under the category of human experimentation and are discussed with great clarity in the Belmont Report, produced in 1976 by the American Department of Health (see chapter 8 for a detailed summary). This report established three basic ethical principles that apply to any procedure that involves humans: respect for persons, beneficence, and informed consent.

Respect for persons in the context of clinical trials demands that subjects enter into research voluntarily and with adequate information. This assumes the individuals are autonomous agents, that is, are competent to make up their own minds. However, there are many instances where potential research subjects are not really autonomous: prisoners, patients in a mental institution, children, the elderly, and the infirm.

Many would argue that human embryos and fetuses should also fall within this category. All these people require special protection to ensure they are not being coerced or fooled into volunteering as research subjects. Beneficence is generally regarded as acts of kindness or charity, but in a research context it is an obligation. It is not enough to respect a potential subject's decisions and to protect them from harm, but in addition, it is necessary to do all that is possible to ensure their well-being. All participants in clinical trials must provide informed consent, in writing. Moreover, steps must be taken to ensure the consent is, in fact, informed. This might involve an independent assessment of the individual's ability to understand the language on the consent form and any instructions or explanations the investigators have given.

The Belmont Report coincides with a growing consensus in the world that human cloning is an unethical form of human experimentation and should not be done. Consequently, legislators around the world have already taken steps to regulate the practice or ban it all together (as discussed in chapter 7). But a confluence of technologies has made cloning the center of a debate that is not specifically addressed by the Belmont Report and may be extremely difficult to resolve. Throughout the 1990s, while Steen Willadsen and Ian Wilmut were laying the foundations for a procedure to clone mammals, other scientists were studying a special kind of cell called a stem cell. These cells are capable of producing any type of cell in the body and hold great promise in the treatment of spinal cord injuries, cardiovascular disease, and devastating neurological diseases such as Parkinson's and Alzheimer's diseases.

Many stem cells can be found in the bone marrow and in the basal layers of the skin, where they serve to regenerate those tissues as they wear out. Other stem cells are found in very young embryos, no more than a day or two old. These cells are also known as embryonic blastomeres. Many scientists believe embryonic stem cells have the greatest plasticity (i.e., ability to form different kinds of cells) of all stem cell types and would like to create an endless supply by a method termed therapeutic cloning. That is, cloning technology would be used to produce human embryos in order to isolate their stem cells. Aside from producing an endless source of these cells, therapeutic cloning has been proposed as a way of providing stem cells to patients without raising the problem of immune rejection. Say, for example, that someone has a spinal cord injury and scientists would like to treat it by injecting stem cells into the site of the injury, where they will differentiate into neurons and, it is hoped, repair the damage. If the stem cells are obtained from a generic lab culture, the cells will be attacked by the patient's immune system, just as any other allograft would be. However, if cells from the patient are cloned, the resulting embryo would be a source of immune-compatible cells that could be injected into the patient without fear of rejection. What is the ethical dilemma here? The embryo has to be killed in order for its cells to be harvested; indeed, the stems cells *are* the embryo. Thus, therapeutic cloning would be used to create a human life so it may die to serve as a source of cells. Killing the embryo is, in effect, an abortion, and this is the potentially explosive mix of technologies at the center of the ethical debate surrounding cloning.

Anti-abortion groups, the Catholic Church, and many people in the general public are strongly opposed to the idea of using human embryos as research subjects and, in particular, are opposed to the idea of creating human life as a disposable source of stem cells. Their objection is based on many of the principles described in the Belmont Report. We take offense at research that uses animals closely related to us, and quite naturally, that offense rises to a maximum when it involves research on humans. Society allows research on human subjects but only because of the policy of informed consent. Embryos cannot give informed consent, but it is safe to assume that if they could, they would choose life over death. In the case of abortion, ethicists and legislators have deferred to the rights of the woman over the rights of the embryo or the fetus. But in the case of therapeutic cloning, there is no such deferral possible, and therefore, within the context of the Belmont Report, there can be no ethical grounds for the production of human embryos as a source of stem cells.

Proponents of therapeutic cloning claim that the medical therapies that could be derived from embryonic stem cells override the ethical problems. However, the Belmont Report, while not specifically addressing the issue of therapeutic cloning, is broad enough to cover ethical issues. Society may agree that giving mice a lethal case of cancer is acceptable if there is a chance it may lead to a cure for humans, but choosing to sacrifice human embryos in order to save other human lives contravenes the intent of the ethical principles established by the report. Some advocates of therapeutic cloning suggest that because the embryos are cloned, they are not really human, and therefore an ethical dilemma does not exist. But other scientists reject the premise that clones are inherently less than, or even different from, their conventionally conceived genetic counterparts. In particular, when Dolly was cloned, Ian Wilmut and many other scientists went to great lengths to assure everyone that Dolly was a normal sheep in every way and that being a clone did not change that. Dolly even went on to bear, by natural means, several healthy lambs and, aside from having her picture published on the cover of *Time* magazine, led a very ordinary life. Consequently, a cloned human embryo deserves the same ethical and legal protection as does a human embryo conceived by natural means.

Advocates of therapeutic cloning, in their eagerness to exploit the properties of embryonic stem cells, have overlooked the great potential of adult stem cells (i.e. stem cells isolated from the bone marrow of adults or from umbilical cord blood). The research of Drs. Catherine Verfaille and Juliet Barker at the University of Minnesota have shown that these cells also possess developmental plasticity and, in the case of bone marrow stem cells, can be harvested from the patients needing treatment, thus eliminating both potential immune rejection and the ethical problems associated with the use of embryos. Developing therapies based on adult stem cells will take longer than it would with embryonic stem cells but avoids the serious ethical problems associated with therapeutic cloning.

The cure of diseases that we face today, like Alzheimer's or cancer, requires very powerful technologies that probe deeply into our cells. Before we consent to using them, however, we must consider whether these techniques compromise what many regard as the essence of our humanity. If we jump for the quick fix, without reflecting on what we believe is right and wrong, we may end up like an old Greek statue: nice to look at, and impervious to disease, but cold as stone.

·7·
LEGAL ISSUES

Dolly's birth, and the perfection of nuclear transfer technology, provided powerful new methods for the production of transgenic animals and for medical therapies. It also introduced many ethical problems that forced governments in Europe and North America to introduce legislation designed to control the use and spread of this technology. The legal issues are focused on two forms of human cloning. The first is reproductive cloning, whereby an embryo is produced by nuclear transfer and then carried to term by a surrogate mother, as was done with Dolly. The second form is known as therapeutic cloning, whereby an embryo is cloned solely for the purpose of harvesting the inner cell mass, or ES cells, for use in a variety of medical therapies. Thus, this form of cloning involves stem cell therapy and has proved to be the most difficult issue to resolve. The legal debate varies from country to country, particularly for therapeutic cloning. We begin by considering the legal issues as they unfolded in the United Kingdom (Britain, Northern Ireland, Wales, and Scotland), for it was there that laws regulating human cloning were first discussed and enacted.

The United Kingdom

The regulation of human cloning in the United Kingdom (U.K.) is governed by the Human Fertilization and Embryology Act of 1990. The legislation, administered by the Human Fertilization and Embryology Authority (HFEA), was enacted to regulate the practice of in vitro fertilization (IVF), which originated in Britain with the birth of the first "test tube" baby, Louise Brown, in 1973. HFEA was established after a great deal of discussion, both inside and outside the British Parliament, that was stimulated by the Committee of Inquiry into Human Fertilization and Embryology. This committee was chaired by Baroness Warnock and was tabled in 1984. The Act of 1990, however, largely implemented the recommendations of the Warnock committee.

Under the Act, research on embryos older than 14 days is prohibited. This time period was set to coincide with the appearance of the primitive streak (an anatomical feature of an embryo that indicates the beginning of neuralation) and the formation of the central nervous system. All research dealing with human embryos is licensed by the HFEA, which may be denied if the authority feels the research objectives may be obtained with nonhuman embryos or by some other means. In general, the license is granted if the research is focused on treatments for infertility, development of contraceptives, or if the results are expected to clarify the causes of miscarriages.

With the birth of Dolly, the HFEA and the Human Genetics Advisory Commission undertook a public consultation on human cloning. Their report, tabled in 1998, recommended that the HFEA issue licenses for therapeutic cloning, and that research involving the embryos so produced would be subject to the 14-day limit imposed by the act for normally, or IVF, conceived embryos. These recommendations were debated at length by the British government and passed into law as the Human Fertilization and Embryology Regulations (HFER) on January 22, 2001. The passage of this law brought with it the concern that some of the cloned embryos might be implanted into a surrogate mother and brought to full term. To ensure that this did not happen, the government introduced the Human Reproductive Cloning bill, which proposed a ban on reproductive cloning. This bill was passed into law on December 4, 2001.

The British legislation covering reproductive and therapeutic cloning is highly regarded around the world, and has served as a model for all subsequent cloning legislation. The legislation regulating therapeutic cloning (HFER 2001) was reviewed by a special committee set up by the House of Lords in 2002. This committee put out a call for evidence from the scientific and research organizations, the churches, medical charities, patients' support groups, pro-life groups, and many organizations representing the general public, such as trades unions and the National Federation of Women's Institutes. The committee received 52 submissions from various organizations, and they held 12 sessions of oral evidence, at which 42 people representing 17 organizations presented their arguments for or against the proposed legislation. Members of the committee also visited research laboratories to gain a better understanding of the science involved. While confirming majority support for HFER 2001, the committee's report called for increased surveillance of therapeutic cloning projects to ensure that every cloned embryo is accounted for, and that the experiments to which the embryos are subjected do not extend beyond what is allowed by law.

The European Union

The European Union (EU), which, until May 1, 2004, included Germany, France, Spain, the Netherlands, and 11 other European countries, agreed with the U.K. position on reproductive cloning and passed laws to ban it. However, the EU strongly disagreed with the U.K. on the issue of therapeutic cloning. Article 18 of the Council of Europe Convention on Human Rights and Biomedicine states categorically that "the creation of human embryos for research purposes is prohibited." Thus therapeutic cloning, or any kind of research that destroys human embryos, is illegal in Germany, Austria, Portugal, Ireland, Norway, and Poland. Even the Netherlands, a politically liberal country, passed a law in 2003 to ban the cloning of human embryos. In addition, the Council of Europe adopted a convention on biomedicine that prohibits the creation of human embryos for research purposes. In 2002 the Netherlands and Sweden appeared willing to allow therapeutic cloning, provided laws were enacted to prohibit placing such embryos in surrogate mothers to be carried to full term. But it became clear that enforcing such a law would be nearly impossible, and so a complete ban on all forms of cloning seemed to be the only practical solution.

The United States

A bill to prohibit all forms of cloning (Human Cloning Prohibition Act of 2001, H.R. 2505), which has the support of President George Bush, was passed by the House of Representatives in July 2001 but has not as yet been written into law. The bill, introduced by Representatives David Weldon (R-Florida) and Bark Stupak (D-Michigan), had a broad base of support but met with opposition when submitted to the Senate for debate in 2002. Dissension came from patient advocate groups and members of the biomedical research community, who agreed to a ban on reproductive cloning but argued in favor of therapeutic cloning. However, neither side could show that they had at least 60 votes needed to bring the bill to a vote. Consequently, the Senate majority leader, Tom Daschle, put the gridlocked issue aside.

In 2003 the House of Representatives took a second vote on the bill, and this time it was approved by an overwhelming margin of 241 to 155. Senator Sam Brownback (R-Kansas) introduced the companion bill to the Senate for debate. Both bills call for a maximum penalty of $1 million in civil fines and up to 10-year jail terms for those who attempt reproductive or therapeutic cloning. Competing legislation was also submitted by Senators Arlen Specter (R-Pennsylvania) and Dianne Feinstein (D-California) that calls for a ban only on reproductive cloning.

In April 2004, 206 members of the U.S. House of Representatives signed a letter urging President Bush to modify his August 2001 executive order limiting federal funds for ES cell research to preexisting cell lines. The letter called for a new policy whereby federal funds would be made available for researchers to create new ES cell lines from embryos left over from in vitro fertilization clinics. On June 4, 58 senators, many of them Republicans, sent a similar letter to the president. However, in response to these letters, Dr. Elias Zerhouni, the director of the National Institutes of Health, and White House spokesman Ken Lisaius reiterated President Bush's position that federal funds should not be used to "encourage further destruction of human embryos that have at least the potential for life."

Legislators debating the cloning bills before the Senate will have to deal with the same question that confronted the U.K. and EU Parliaments in 2001: Namely, does a five-day-old embryo qualify for legal protection or does it not? U.K. legislation holds that an embryo less than 14 days old does not qualify, whereas a 15-day-old embryo does. The EU voted overwhelming support for a complete ban on human cloning, and it reiterated this decision in April 2003. Firm support for a total ban on human cloning from the EU, and the perceived difficulties of regulating the use of cloned embryos, will likely influence the outcome of the vote in the Senate. In addition, new research on adult stem cells and umbilical cord blood stem cells indicate that they have the same potential for curing disease as do ES cells. Thus the argument that therapeutic cloning and ES cells are essential for the development of effective stem cell therapies is no longer convincing.

.8.

RESOURCE CENTER

Eukaryote Cell Primer

Life on Earth began 3.5 billion years ago in the form of single cells that appeared in the oceans. These cells evolved into ancestral prokaryotes and, about 2 billion years ago, gave rise to Archaea, bacteria, and eukaryotes, the three major divisions of life in the world. Eukaryotes, in turn, gave rise to plants, animals, protozoans, and fungi. Each of these groups represents a distinct phylogenetic kingdom. The Archaea and bacteria represent a fifth kingdom, known as the monera or prokaryotes. Archaea and bacteria are very similar anatomically, both lacking a true nucleus and internal organelles. A prokaryote genome is a single, circular piece of naked DNA, called a chromosome, containing fewer than 5,000 genes. Eukaryotes (meaning "true nuclei") are much more complex, having many membrane-bounded organelles. These include a nucleus, nucleolus, endoplasmic reticulum (ER), Golgi complex, mitochondria, lysosomes, and peroxisomes.

The eukaryote nucleus, bounded by a double phospholipid membrane, contains a DNA (deoxyribonucleic acid) genome on two or more linear chromosomes, each of which may contain up to 10,000 genes. The nucleus also contains an assembly plant for ribosomal subunits, called the nucleolus. The endoplasmic reticulum (ER) and the Golgi complex work together to glycosylate proteins and lipids (attach sugar molecules to the proteins and lipids producing glycoproteins and glycolipids), most of which are destined for the cell membrane to form a molecular "forest" known as the glycocalyx. The glycoproteins and

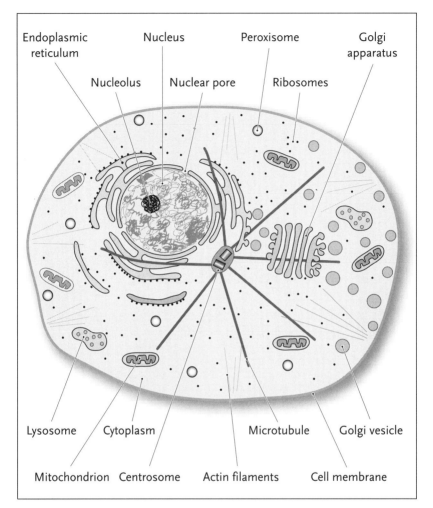

The eukaryote cell. The structural components shown here are present in organisms as diverse as protozoans, plants, and animals. The nucleus contains the DNA genome and an assembly plant for ribosomal subunits (the nucleolus). The endoplasmic reticulum (ER) and the Golgi work together to modify proteins, most of which are destined for the cell membrane. These proteins are sent to the membrane in Golgi vesicles. Mitochondria provide the cell with energy in the form of ATP. Ribosomes, some of which are attached to the ER, synthesize proteins. Lysosomes and peroxisomes recycle cellular material and molecules. The microtubules and centrosome form the spindle apparatus for moving chromosomes to the daughter cells during cell division. Actin filaments and a weblike structure consisting of intermediate filaments (not shown) form the cytoskeleton.

glycolipids travel from the ER to the Golgi, and from the Golgi to the cell surface, in membrane-bounded vesicles that form by budding off the organelle by exocytosis. Thus the cytoplasm contains many transport vesicles that originate from the ER and Golgi. The Golgi vesicles bud off the outer chamber, or the one farthest from the ER. Mitochondria, once free-living prokaryotes, and the only other organelle with a double membrane, provide the cell with energy in the form of adenosine triphosphate (ATP). The production of ATP is carried out by an assembly of metal-containing proteins, called the electron transport chain, located in the mitochondrion inner membrane. Ribosomes, some of which are attached to the ER, synthesize proteins. Lysosomes and peroxisomes recycle cellular material and molecules. The microtubules and centrosome form the spindle apparatus for moving chromosomes to the daughter cells during cell division. Actin filaments and a weblike structure consisting of intermediate filaments form the cytoskeleton.

MOLECULES OF THE CELL

Cells are biochemical entities that synthesize many thousands of molecules. Studying these chemicals, and the biochemistry of the cell, would be a daunting task were it not for the fact that most of the chemical variation is based on six types of molecules that are assembled into just four types of macromolecules. The six basic molecules are amino acids, phosphate, glycerol, sugars, fatty acids, and nucleotides. Amino acids have a simple core structure consisting of an amino group, a carboxyl group, and a variable R group attached to a carbon atom. There are 20 different kinds of amino acids, each with a unique R group. Phosphates are extremely important molecules that are used in the construction or modification of many other molecules. They are also used to store chemical-bond energy. Glycerol is a simple, three-carbon alcohol that is an important component of cell membranes and fat reservoirs. Sugars are extremely versatile molecules that are used as an energy source and for structural purposes. Glucose, a six-carbon sugar, is the primary energy source for most cells, and it is the principal sugar used to glycosylate proteins and lipids for the production of the glycocalyx. Plants have exploited the structural potential of sugars in their production of cellulose, and thus wood, bark, grasses, and reeds are polymers of glucose and other monosaccharides. Ribose, a five-carbon sugar, is a

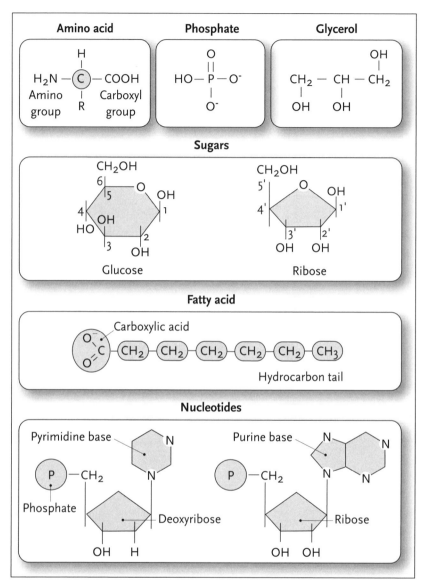

Molecules of the cell. Amino acids are the building blocks for proteins. Phosphate is an important component of many other molecules and is added to proteins to modify their behavior. Glycerol is a three-carbon alcohol that is an important ingredient in cell membranes and fat. Sugars, like glucose, are a primary energy source for most cells and also have many structural functions. Fatty acids are involved in the production of cell membranes and storage of fat. Nucleotides are the building blocks for DNA and RNA.

component of nucleic acids as well as of ATP. The numbering convention for sugar carbon atoms is shown in the figure on page 81. Ribose carbons are numbered as 1' (1 prime), 2', and so on. Consequently, references to nucleic acids, which include ribose, often refer to the 3' or 5' carbon. Fatty acids consist of a carboxyl group (when ionized it becomes a carboxylic acid) linked to a hydrophobic hydrocarbon tail. These molecules are used in the construction of cell membranes and fat. Nucleotides are building blocks for DNA and RNA (ribonucleic acid). Nucleotides consist of three components: a phosphate, a ribose sugar, and a nitrogenous (nitrogen-containing) ring compound that behaves as a base in solution. Nucleotide bases appear in two forms: a single-ring nitrogenous base, called a pyrimidine, and a double-ringed base, called a purine. There are two kinds of purines (adenine and guanine) and three pyrimidines (uracil, cytosine, and thymine). Uracil is specific to RNA, substituting for thymine. In addition, RNA nucleotides contain ribose, whereas DNA nucleotides contain deoxyribose (hence the origin of their names). Ribose has a hydroxyl (OH) group attached to both the 2' and 3' carbons, whereas deoxyribose is missing the 2' hydroxyl group. ATP, the molecule used by all cells as a source of energy, is a ribose nucleotide consisting of the purine base adenine and three phosphates attached to the 5' carbon of the ribose sugar. The phosphates are labeled α (alpha), β (beta), and γ (gamma), and are linked to the carbon in a tandem order, beginning with α. The energy stored by this molecule is carried by the covalent bonds of the β and γ phosphates. Breaking these bonds sequentially releases the energy they contain while converting ATP to adenosine diphosphate (ADP) and then to adenosine monophosphate (AMP). AMP is converted back to ATP by mitochondria.

MACROMOLECULES OF THE CELL

The six basic molecules are used by all cells to construct five essential macromolecules. These include proteins, RNA, DNA, phospholipids, and sugar polymers, known as polysaccharides. Amino acids are linked together by peptide bonds to construct a protein. A peptide bond is formed by linking the carboxyl end of one amino acid to the amino end of second amino acid. Thus, once constructed, every protein has an amino end and a carboxyl end. An average protein may

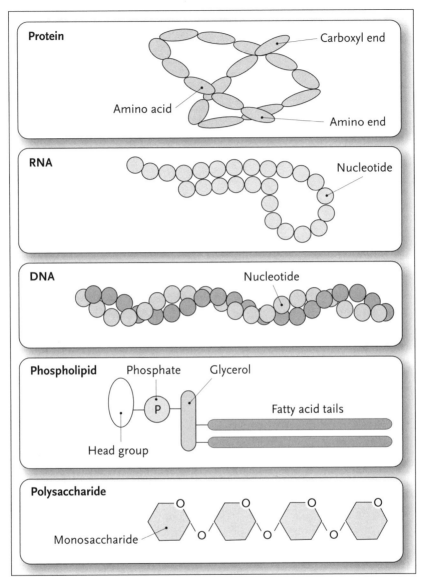

Macromolecules of the cell. Protein is made from amino acids linked together to form a long chain that can fold up into a three-dimensional structure. RNA and DNA are long chains of nucleotides. RNA is generally single stranded but can form localized double-stranded regions. DNA is a double-stranded helix, with one strand coiling around the other. A phospholipid is composed of a hydrophilic head-group, a phosphate, a glycerol molecule, and two hydrophobic fatty acid tails. Polysaccharides are sugar polymers.

consist of 300 to 400 amino acids. Nucleic acids are macromolecules constructed from nucleotides. The 5' phosphate of one nucleotide is linked to the 3' OH of a second nucleotide. Additional nucleotides are always linked to the 3' OH of the last nucleotide in the chain. Consequently, the growth of the chain is said to be in the 5' to 3' direction. RNA nucleotides are adenine, uracil, cytosine, and guanine. A typical RNA molecule consists of 2,000 to 3,000 nucleotides; it is generally single stranded but can form localized double-stranded regions. RNA is involved in the synthesis of proteins and is a structural and enzymatic component of ribosomes. DNA, a double-stranded nucleic acid, encodes cellular genes and is constructed from

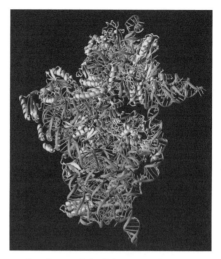

Molecule model of the 30S ribosomal subunit, which consists of protein (light gray corkscrew structures) and RNA (coiled ladders). The overall shape of the molecule is determined by the RNA that is also responsible for the catalytic function of the ribosome. *(Courtesy of V. Ramakrishnan, MRC Laboratory of Molecular Biology, Cambridge)*

adenine, thymine, cytosine, and guanine deoxyribonucleotides (dATP, dTTP, dCTP, and dGTP, where "d" indicates deoxyribose). The two DNA strands coil around each other like strands in piece of rope, and for this reason the molecule is known as the double helix. DNA is an extremely large macromolecule, typically consisting of more than a million nucleotide pairs (or base pairs). Double-stranded DNA forms when two chains of nucleotides interact through the formation of chemical bonds between complementary base pairs. The chemistry of the bases is such that adenine pairs with thymine, and cytosine pairs with guanine. For stability, the two strands are antiparallel, that is, the orientation of one strand is in the 5' to 3' direction, while the complementary strand runs 3' to 5'. Phospholipids, the main component of cell membranes, are composed of a polar head group (usually an alcohol), a phosphate, glycerol, and two hydrophobic fatty acid tails. Fat that is stored in the body as an energy reserve has a structure similar to a phospholipid, being composed of three fatty acid chains attached to a molecule of glycerol. The third fatty acid takes the place of

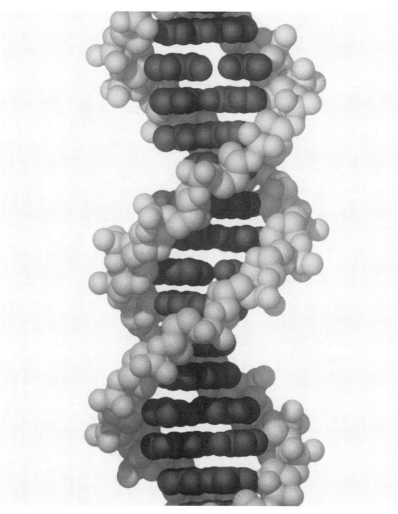

Computer model of DNA. The two strands coil around each other to form a helix that, when looking down on it from above, coils to the right. The spherical structures in this image represent the various atoms in the sugars and bases (dark gray) and phosphates (light gray). *(Kenneth Edward/BioGrafx/ Photo Researchers, Inc.)*

the phosphate and head-group of a phospholipid. Sugars are polymerized to form chains of two or more monosaccharides. Disaccharides (two monosaccharides) and oligosaccharides (three to 12 monosaccharides) are attached to proteins and lipids destined for the glycocalyx. Polysaccharides, such as glycogen and starch, may contain several hundred monosaccharides and are stored in cells as an energy reserve.

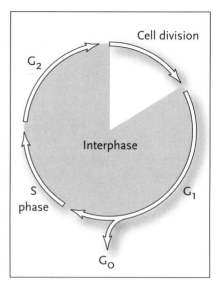

The cell cycle. Most cells spend their time cycling between a state of calm (interphase) and cell division. Interphase is further divided into three subphases: Gap 1 (G_1), S phase (DNA synthesis), and Gap 2 (G_2). Cells may exit the cycle by entering a special phase called G_0.

THE CELL CYCLE

Cells inherited the power of reproduction from prebiotic bubbles that split in half at regular intervals under the influence of the turbulent environment that characterized the Earth more than 3 billion years ago. This pattern of turbulent fragmentation followed by a brief period of calm is now a regular behavior pattern of every cell. Even today, after 3 billion years, many cells still divide every 20 minutes.

The regular alternation between division and calm has come to be known as the cell cycle. In studying this cycle, scientists have recognized different states of calm and different ways in which a cell can divide. The calm state of the cell cycle, referred to as interphase, is divided into three subphases called Gap 1 (G_1), S phase (a period of DNA synthesis), and Gap 2 (G_2). The conclusion of interphase, and with it the termination of G_2, occurs with division of the cell and a return to G_1. Cells may leave the cycle by entering a special phase called G_0. Some cells, such as postmitotic neurons in an animal's brain, remain in G_0 for the life of the organism.

Although interphase is a period of relative calm, the cell grows continuously during this period, working hard to prepare for the next round of division. Two notable events are the duplication of the spindle (the centrosome and associated microtubules), a structure that is crucial for the movement of the chromosomes during cell division, and the appearance of an enzyme called maturation promoting factor (MPF) at the end of G_2. MPF phosphorylates histones. The histones are proteins that bind to the DNA, which when phosphorylated, compact (or condense) the chromosomes in preparation for cell division. MPF is also responsible for the breakdown of the nuclear membrane. When cell division is complete, MPF disappears, allowing the chromosomes to decondense and the nuclear envelope to reform. Completion of a normal cell cycle always involves the division of a cell into two daughter cells. This can occur by a process known as mitosis, which is intended for cell multiplication, and by second process known as meiosis, which is intended for sexual reproduction.

MITOSIS

Mitosis is used by all free-living eukaryotes (protozoans) as a means of asexual reproduction. The growth of a plant or an animal is also accomplished with this form of cell division. Mitosis is divided into four stages: prophase, metaphase, anaphase, and telophase. All these stages are marked out in accordance with the behavior of the nucleus and the chromosomes. Prophase marks the period during which the duplicated chromosomes begin condensation, and the two centrosomes begin moving to opposite poles of the cell. Under the microscope, the chromosomes become visible as X-shaped structures, which are the two duplicated chromosomes, often called sister chromatids. A special region of each chromosome, called a centromere, holds the chromatids together. Proteins bind to the centromere to form a structure called the kinetochore. Metaphase is a period during which the chromosomes are sorted out and aligned between the two centrosomes. By this time, the nuclear membrane has completely broken down. The two centrosomes and the microtubules fanning out between them form the mitotic spindle. The area in between the spindles, where the chromosomes are aligned, is often referred to as the metaphase plate. Some of the microtubules make contact with the kinetochores, while others

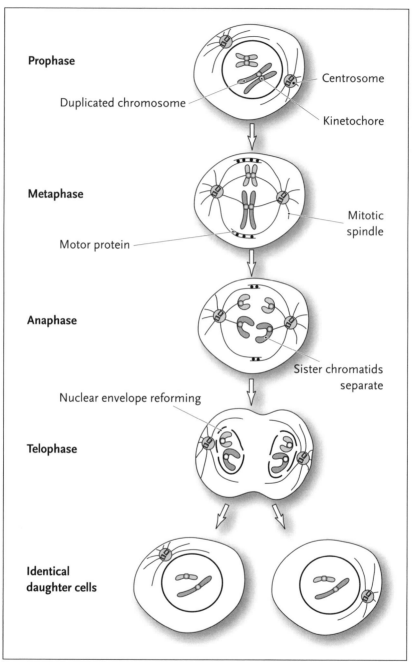

Mitosis. Principal stages dealing with the movement and partitioning of the chromosomes between the future daughter cells. For clarity, only two chromosomes are shown.

overlap, with motor proteins situated in between. Eukaryotes are normally diploid, so a cell would have two copies of each chromosome, one from the mother and one from the father. Anaphase is characterized by the movement of the duplicated chromosomes to opposite poles of the cell. The first step is the release of an enzyme that breaks the bonds holding the kinetochores together, thus allowing the sister chromatids to separate from each other while remaining bound to their respective microtubules. Motor proteins then move along the microtubule, dragging the chromosomes to opposite ends of the cell. Using energy supplied by ATP, the motor proteins break the microtubule down as it drags the chromosome along so that the microtubule is gone by the time the chromosome reaches the spindle pole. Throughout this process, the motor proteins and the chromosome manage to stay one step ahead of the disintegrating microtubule. The overlapping microtubules aid movement of the chromosomes toward the poles as another type of motor protein pushes the microtubules in opposite directions, effectively forcing the centrosomes toward the poles. This accounts for the greater overlap of microtubules in metaphase as compared with anaphase. During telophase, the daughter chromosomes arrive at the spindle poles and decondense to form the relaxed chromatin characteristic of interphase nuclei. The nuclear envelope begins forming around the chromosomes, marking the end of mitosis. During the same period, a contractile ring, made of the proteins myosin and actin, begins pinching the parental cell in two. This stage, separate from mitosis, is called cytokinesis and leads to the formation of two daughter cells, each with one nucleus.

MEIOSIS

Unlike mitosis, which leads to the growth of an organism, meiosis is intended for sexual reproduction and occurs exclusively in ovaries and testes. Eukaryotes, being diploid, receive chromosomes from both parents; if gametes were produced using mitosis, a catastrophic growth in the number of chromosomes would occur each time a sperm fertilized an egg. Meiosis is a special form of cell division that produces haploid gametes (eggs and sperm), each processing half as many chromosomes as the diploid cell. When haploid gametes fuse, they produce an embryo with the correct number of chromosomes.

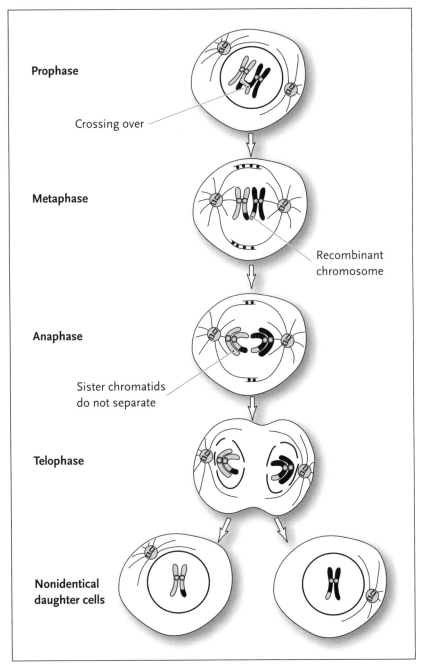

Prophase

Crossing over

Metaphase

Recombinant
chromosome

Anaphase

Sister chromatids
do not separate

Telophase

**Nonidentical
daughter cells**

Meiosis I. The most notable features include genetic recombination (crossing over) between the homologous chromosomes during prophase, comigration of the sister chromatids during anaphase, and the production of nonidentical daughter cells. Only one homologous pair is shown.

The existence of meiosis was first suggested 100 years ago when microbiologists counted the number of chromosomes in somatic and germ cells. The roundworm, for example, was found to have four chromosomes in its somatic cells but only two in its gametes. Many other studies also compared the amount of DNA in nuclei from somatic cells and gonads, always with the same result: The amount of DNA in somatic cells is exactly double the amount in fully mature gametes. To understand how this could be, scientists studied cell division in the gonads and were able to show that meiosis occurs as two rounds of cell division with only one round of DNA synthesis. The two rounds of division were called meiosis I and meiosis II, and scientists observed that both could be divided into the same four stages known to occur in mitosis. Indeed, meiosis II is virtually identical to a mitotic division. Meiosis I resembles mitosis, but close examination shows three important differences: gene swapping occurs between homologous chromosomes in prophase; homologs (i.e., two homologous chromosomes) remain paired at metaphase, instead of lining up at the plate as is done in mitosis; and the kinetochores do not separate at anaphase.

Homologous chromosomes are two identical chromosomes that come from different parents. For example, humans have 23 chromosomes from the father and the same 23 from the mother. We each have a maternal chromosome 1 and a paternal chromosome 1; they carry the same genes but specify slightly different traits. Chromosome 1 may carry the gene for eye color, but the maternal version, or allele, may specify blue eyes, whereas the paternal allele specifies brown. During prophase, homologous pairs exchange large numbers of genes by swapping whole pieces of chromosome. Thus one of the maternal chromatids (gray in the figure on page 90) ends up with a piece of paternal chromosome, and a paternal chromatid receives the corresponding piece of maternal chromosome. Mixing genetic material in this way is unique to meiosis, and it is one of the reasons sexual reproduction has been such a powerful evolutionary force.

During anaphase of meiosis I, the kinetochores do not separate as they do in mitosis. The effect of this is to separate the maternal and paternal chromosomes by sending them to different daughter cells, although the segregation is random. That is, the daughter cells receive a random assortment of maternal and paternal chromosomes, rather than one daughter cell receiving all paternal chromosomes and the other all maternal chromosomes. Random segregation, along with genetic recombination, accounts for the fact that while children resemble their parents, they do not look or act exactly like them. These two mechanisms are responsible for the remarkable adaptability of all eukaryotes. Meiosis II begins immediately after the completion of meiosis I, which produces two daughter cells each containing a duplicated parent chromosome and a recombinant chromosome consisting of both paternal and maternal DNA. These two cells divide mitotically to produce four haploid cells, each of which is genetically unique, containing unaltered or recombinant maternal and paternal chromosomes. Meiosis produces haploid cells by passing through two rounds of cell division with only one round of DNA synthesis. However, as we have seen, the process is not just concerned with reducing the number of chromosomes but is also involved in stirring up the genetic pot in order to produce unique gametes that may someday give rise to an equally unique individual.

DNA REPLICATION

DNA replication, which occurs during the S phase of the cell cycle, requires the coordinated effort of a team of enzymes, led by DNA helicase and primase. The helicase is a remarkable enzyme that is responsible for separating the two DNA strands, a feat that it accomplishes at an astonishing rate of 1,000 nucleotides every second. This enzyme gets its name from the fact that it unwinds the DNA helix as it separates the two strands. The enzyme responsible for reading the template strand, and for synthesizing the new daughter strand, is called DNA polymerase. This enzyme reads the parental DNA in the 3' to 5' direction and creates a daughter strand that grows 5' to 3'. DNA polymerase also has an editorial function, in that it checks the preceding nucleotide to make sure it is correct before it adds a nucleotide to the growing chain. The editor function of this enzyme introduces an interesting problem: How can the polymerase add the very first nucleotide, when it has to check a preceding nucleotide before adding a new one? A special enzyme, called primase, which is attached to the helicase, solves this problem. Primase synthesizes short pieces of RNA that forms a DNA-RNA double-stranded region. The RNA becomes a temporary part of the daughter

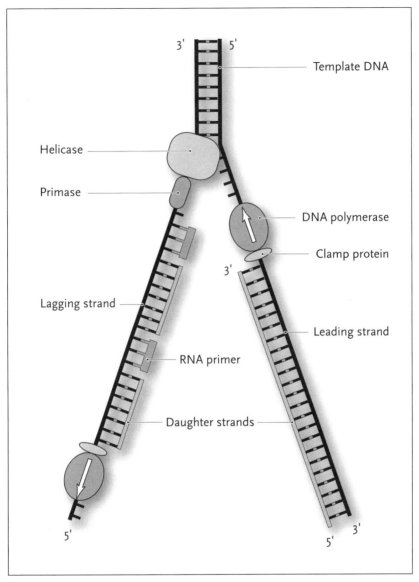

3'   5'

Template DNA

Helicase

Primase

DNA polymerase

Clamp protein

3'

Lagging strand

Leading strand

RNA primer

Daughter strands

5'

5'   3'

DNA replication. The helicase separates the two strands so the DNA polymerase can synthesize new strands. The primase provides replication signals for the polymerase, in the form of RNA primers, and the clamp protein keeps the polymerase from falling off the DNA. The leading strand requires only a single primer (not shown). The lagging strand requires many primers, and the daughter strand is synthesized as a series of DNA fragments that are later joined into one continuous strand.

strand, thus priming the DNA polymerase by providing the crucial first nucleotide in the new strand. Once the chromosome is duplicated, DNA repair enzymes remove the RNA primers and replace them with DNA nucleotides.

TRANSCRIPTION, TRANSLATION, AND THE GENETIC CODE

Genes encode proteins and several kinds of RNA. Extracting the information from DNA requires the processes of transcription and translation. Transcription, catalyzed by the enzyme RNA polymerase, copies one strand of the DNA into a complementary strand of messenger RNA (mRNA) or ribosomal RNA (rRNA) that is used in the construction of ribosomes. Messenger RNA translocates to the cytoplasm, where it is translated into a protein by ribosomes. Newly transcribed rRNA is sent to the nucleolus for ribosome assembly and is never translated. Ribosomes are complex structures consisting of about 50 proteins and four kinds of rRNA, known as 5S, 5.8S, 18S, and 28S rRNA (the "S" refers to a sedimentation coefficient that is proportional to size). These RNAs range in size from about 500 bases up to 2,000 bases for the 28S. The ribosome is assembled in the nucleolus as two nonfunctional subunits before being sent out to the cytoplasm where they combine, along with an mRNA, to form a fully functional unit. The production of ribosomes in this way ensures that translation never occurs in the nucleus.

The genetic code provides a way for the translation machinery to interpret the sequence information stored in the DNA molecule and represented by mRNA. DNA is a linear sequence of four different kinds of nucleotides, so the simplest code could be one in which each nucleotide specifies a different amino acid, that is, adenine coding for the amino acid glycine, cytosine for lysine, and so on. The first cells may have used this coding system, but it is limited to the construction of proteins consisting of only four different kinds of amino acids. Eventually, a more elaborate code evolved in which a combination of three out of the four possible DNA nucleotides, called codons, specifies a single amino acid. With this scheme, it is possible to have a unique code for each of the 20 naturally occurring amino acids. For example, the codon AGC specifies the amino acid serine, whereas TGC specifies the amino acid cysteine. Thus, a gene may be viewed as a long continuous

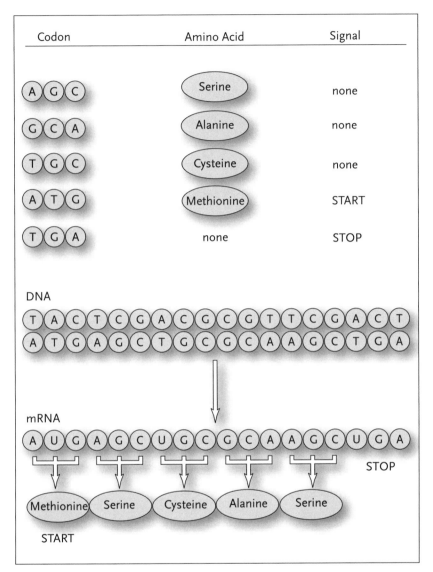

Transcription, translation, and the genetic code. Five codons are shown, four specifying amino acids (protein subunits) and two of the five serving as start and stop signals. The codons, including the start and stop signals, are linked together to form a gene on the bottom, or coding, DNA strand. The coding strand is copied into messenger RNA (mRNA), which is used to synthesize the protein. Nucleotides appear as round beads: adenine (A), thymine (T), cytosine (C), and guanine (G). Amino acids appear as labeled elliptical beads. Note that in mRNA, uracil (U) replaces the thymine (T) found in DNA.

sequence of codons. However, not all codons specify an amino acid. The sequence TGA signals the end of the gene, and a special codon, ATG, signals the start site, in addition to specifying the amino acid methionine. Consequently, all proteins begin with this amino acid, although it is sometimes removed once construction of the protein is complete. As mentioned above, an average protein may consist of 300 to 400 amino acids; since the codon consists of three nucleotides for each amino acid, a typical gene may be 900 to 1,200 nucleotides long.

POWER GENERATION

ATP is produced in mitochondria from AMP, or ADP, and phosphate (PO_4). This process involves a number of metal-binding proteins, called the respiratory chain (also known as the electron transport chain), and a special ion channel-enzyme called ATP synthetase. The respiratory chain consists of three major components: NADH dehydrogenase, cytochrome b, and cytochrome oxidase. All these components are protein complexes that have an iron (NADH dehydrogenase, cytochrome b) or a copper core (cytochrome oxidase), and together with the ATP synthetase are located in the inner membrane of the mitochondria.

The respiratory chain is analogous to an electric cable that transports electricity from a hydroelectric dam to our homes, where it is used to turn on lights or run our stereos. The human body, like that of all animals, generates electricity by processing food molecules through a metabolic pathway, called the Krebs cycle. The electricity, or electrons so generated, travel through the respiratory chain, and as they do, they power the synthesis of ATP. All electric circuits must have a ground, that is, the electrons need someplace to go once they have completed the circuit. In the case of the respiratory chain, the ground is oxygen. After passing through the chain, the electrons are picked up by oxygen, which combines with hydrogen ions to form water.

THE GLYCOCALYX

This structure is an enormously diverse collection of glycoproteins and glycolipids that covers the surface of every cell, like trees on the surface of the Earth, and has many important functions. All eukaryotes originated from free-living cells that hunted bacteria for food. The glycocalyx evolved to meet the demands of this kind of lifestyle, providing a way for the cell to locate, capture, and ingest food molecules or prey organisms. Cell-surface glycoproteins also form transporters and ion channels that serve as gateways into the cell. Neurons have refined ion channels for the purpose of cell-to-cell communication, giving rise to

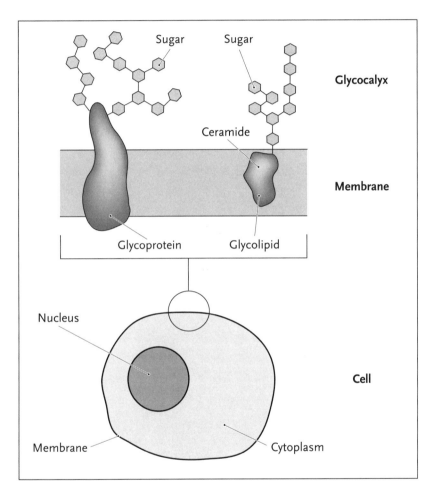

The eukaryote glycocalyx. The eukaryote's molecular forest consists of glycoproteins and glycolipids. Two examples are shown at the top, a glycoprotein on the left and a glycolipid on the right. The glycoprotein trees have "trunks" made of protein and "leaves" made of sugar molecules. Glycolipids also have "leaves" made of sugar molecules, but the "trunks" are a fatty compound called ceramide that is completely submerged within the plane of the membrane. The glycocalyx has many jobs, including cell-to-cell communication, and the transport and detection of food molecules. It also provides recognition markers so the immune system can detect foreign cells.

the nervous systems found in most animal species. In higher vertebrates, certain members of the glycocalyx are used by cells of the
immune system as recognition markers to detect invading microbes or
foreign cells introduced as an organ or tissue transplant.

Recombinant DNA Primer

Recombinant technology is a collection of procedures that make it possible to isolate a gene and produce enough of it for a detailed study of its
structure and function. Central to this technology is the ability to construct libraries of DNA fragments that represent the genetic repertoire
of an entire organism or of a specific cell type. Constructing these
libraries involves splicing different pieces of DNA together to form a
novel or recombinant genetic entity, from which the procedure derives its
name. DNA cloning and library construction were made possible by the
discovery of DNA-modifying enzymes that can seal two pieces of DNA
together or can cut DNA at sequence-specific sites. Many of the procedures that are part of recombinant technology, such as DNA sequencing
or filter hybridization, were developed in order to characterize DNA
fragments that were isolated from cells or gene libraries. Obtaining the
sequence of a gene has made it possible to study the organization of the
genome, but more important, it has provided a simple way of determining the protein sequence and the expression profile for any gene.

DNA-MODIFYING ENZYMES

Two of the most important enzymes used in recombinant technology
are those that can modify DNA by sealing two fragments together and
others that can cut DNA at specific sites. The first modifying enzyme to
be discovered was DNA ligase, an enzyme that can join two pieces of
DNA together and is an important component of the cell's DNA replication and repair machinery. Other DNA-modifying enzymes, called
restriction enzymes, cut DNA at sequence-specific sites, with different
members of the family cutting at different sites. Restriction enzymes are
isolated from bacteria, and since their discovery in 1970, more than 90
such enzymes have been isolated from more than 230 bacterial strains.

The name "restriction enzyme" is cryptic and calls for an explana-
tion. During the period when prokaryotes began to appear on Earth,

their environment contained a wide assortment of molecules that were released into the soil or water by other cells, either deliberately or when the cells died. DNA of varying lengths was among these molecules and was readily taken up by living cells. If the foreign DNA contained complete genes from a competing bacterial species, there was the real possibility that those genes could have been transcribed and translated by the host cell with potentially fatal results. As a precaution, prokaryotes evolved a set of enzymes that would *restrict* the foreign DNA population by cutting it up into smaller pieces before being broken down completely to individual nucleotides.

GEL ELECTROPHORESIS

This procedure is used to separate different DNA and RNA fragments in a slab of agar or polyacrylamide subjected to an electric field. Nucleic acids carry a negative charge and thus will migrate toward a positively charged electrode. The gel acts as a sieving medium that impedes the movement of the molecules. Thus the rate at which the fragments migrate is a function of their size; small fragments migrate more rapidly than large fragments. The gel, containing the samples, is run submerged in a special pH-regulated solution, or buffer, containing a nucleic acid–specific dye, ethidium bromide. This dye produces a strong reddish-yellow fluorescence when exposed to ultraviolet (UV) radiation. Consequently, after electrophoresis, the nucleic acid can be detected by photographing the gel under UV illumination.

DNA CLONING

In 1973 scientists discovered that restriction enzymes, DNA ligase, and bacterial plasmids could be used to clone DNA molecules. Plasmids are small (about 4,000 base pairs, also expressed as 4.0 kilo base pairs or 4 Kbp) circular minichromosomes that occur naturally in bacteria and are often exchanged between cells by passive diffusion. When a bacterium acquires a new plasmid, it is said to have been transfected. For bacteria, the main advantage to swapping plasmids is that they often carry antibiotic resistance genes, so that a cell sensitive to ampicillin can become resistant simply by acquiring the right plasmid.

The first cloning experiment used a plasmid from *Escherichia coli* that was cut with the restriction enzyme *Eco*RI. The plasmid had a

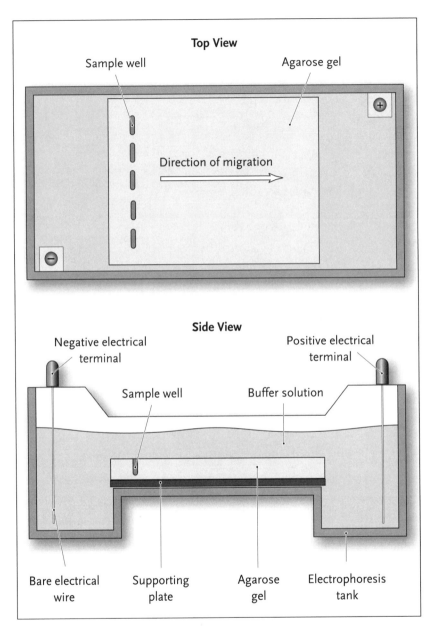

Agarose gel electrophoresis. An agarose gel is placed in an electrophoresis tank and submerged in a buffer solution. The electrical terminals are connected to a power source, with the sample wells positioned near the negative terminal. When the current is turned on, the negatively charged nucleic acids migrate toward the positive terminal. The migration rate is an inverse function of molecular size. (Large molecules travel slower than small ones.)

single *Eco*RI site so the restriction enzyme simply opened the circular molecule, rather than cutting it up into many useless pieces. Foreign DNA, cut with the same restriction enzyme, was incubated with the

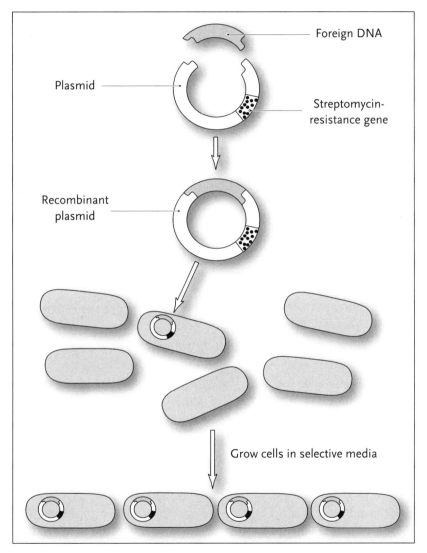

Cloning DNA in a plasmid. The foreign DNA and the plasmid are cut with the same restriction enzyme, allowed to fuse, and then sealed with DNA ligase. The recombinant plasmid is mixed with bacterial cells, some of which pick up the plasmid, allowing them to grow in a culture medium containing the antibiotic streptomycin. The bacteria's main chromosome is not shown.

plasmid. Because the plasmid and foreign DNA were both cut with *Eco*RI, the DNA could insert itself into the plasmid to form a hybrid, or recombinant plasmid, after which DNA ligase sealed the two together. The reaction mixture was added to a small volume of *E. coli* so that some of the cells could take up the recombinant plasmid before being transferred to a nutrient broth containing streptomycin. Only those cells carrying the recombinant plasmid, which contained an anti-streptomycin gene, could grow in the presence of this antibiotic. Each time the cells divided, the plasmid DNA was duplicated along with the main chromosome. After the cells had grown overnight, the foreign DNA had been amplified, or cloned, billions of times and was easily isolated for sequencing or expression studies.

GENOMIC AND cDNA LIBRARIES

The basic cloning procedure described above not only provides a way to amplify a specific piece of DNA, but it can also be used to construct gene libraries. In this case, however, the cloning vector is a bacteriophage, called lambda. The lambda genome is double-stranded linear DNA of about 40 Kbp, much of which can be replaced by foreign DNA without sacrificing the ability of the virus to infect bacteria. This is the great advantage of lambda over a plasmid. Lambda can accommodate very long pieces of DNA, often long enough to contain an entire gene, whereas a plasmid cannot accommodate foreign DNA that is larger than 4 Kbp. Moreover, bacteriophages have the natural ability to infect bacteria, so that the efficiency of transfection is 100 times greater than it is for plasmids.

The construction of a gene library begins by isolating genomic DNA and digesting it with a restriction enzyme to produce fragments of 1,000 to 10,000 base pairs. These fragments are ligated into lambda genomes, which are subjected to a packaging reaction to produce mature viral particles, most of which carry a different piece of the genomic DNA. This collection of viruses is called a genomic library and is used to study the structure and organization of specific genes. Clones from a library such as this contain the coding sequences, in addition to introns, intervening sequences, promoters, and enhancers. An alternative form of a gene library can be constructed by isolating mRNA from a specific cell type. This RNA is converted to the complementary DNA (cDNA) using an RNA-dependent DNA polymerase called reverse transcriptase. The cDNA is ligated to lambda genomes and packaged as for the genomic library. This collection of recombinant viruses is a cDNA library and only contains genes that were being expressed by the cells when the RNA was extracted. It does not include introns or controlling elements, as these are lost during transcription and the processing that occurs in the cell to make mature mRNA. Thus a cDNA library is intended for the purpose of studying gene expression and the structure of the coding region only.

LABELING CLONED DNA

Many of the procedures used in the area of recombinant technology were inspired by the events that occur during DNA replication. This includes the labeling of cloned DNA for use as probes in expression studies, DNA sequencing, and polymerase chain reaction (PCR, described in a following section). DNA replication involves duplicating one of the strands (the parent, or template strand) by linking nucleotides in an order specified by the template and depends on a large number of enzymes, the most important of which is DNA polymerase. This enzyme, guided by the template strand, constructs a daughter strand by linking nucleotides together. One such nucleotide is deoxyadenine triphosphate (dATP). Deoxyribonucleotides have a single hydroxyl group located at the 3' carbon of the sugar group while the triphosphate is attached to the 5' carbon. The procedure for labeling DNA probes, developed in 1983, introduces radioactive nucleotides into a DNA molecule. This method supplies DNA polymerase with a single-stranded DNA template, a primer, and the four nucleotides in a buffered solution to induce in vitro replication. The daughter strand, which becomes the probe, is labeled by including a nucleotide in the reaction mix that is linked to a radioactive isotope. The radioactive nucleotide is usually deoxycytosine triphosphate (dCTP), or dATP.

Single-stranded DNA hexamers (six bases long) are used as primers, and these are produced in such a way that they contain all possible permutations of four bases taken six at a time. Randomizing the base sequence for the primers ensures there will be at least one primer site in a template that is only 50 bp long. Templates used in labeling reactions such as this are generally 100 to 800 bp long. This strategy of labeling DNA, known as random primer or oligo labeling, is widely used in cloning and in DNA and RNA filter hybridizations (described in following sections).

DNA SEQUENCING

A sequencing reaction developed by the British biochemist Dr. Fred Sanger in 1976 is another technique that takes its inspiration from the natural process of DNA replication. DNA polymerase requires a primer with a free 3' hydroxyl group. The polymerase adds the first nucleotide to this group, and all subsequent bases are added to the 3' hydroxyl of the previous base. Sequencing by the Sanger method is usually performed with the DNA cloned into a plasmid. This simplifies the choice of the initial primers because their sequence can be derived from the known plasmid sequence. An engineered plasmid primer site adjacent to a cloned DNA fragment is shown in the figure on DNA sequencing. Once the primer binds to the primer site, the cloned DNA may be replicated. Sanger's innovation involved the synthesis of artificial nucleotides lacking the 3' hydroxyl group, thus producing dideoxynucleotides (ddATP, ddCTP, ddGTP, and ddTTP). Incorporation of a dideoxynucleotide terminates the growth of the daughter strand at that point, and this can be used to determine the size of each daughter strand. The shortest daughter strand represents the

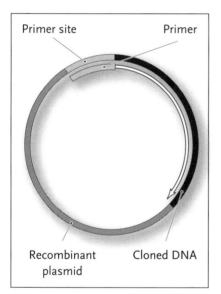

Plasmid primer site for DNA sequencing. The cloned DNA is inserted into the plasmid near an engineered primer site. Once the primer binds to the primer site, the cloned DNA may be replicated, as part of a sequencing reaction, in the direction indicated by the arrow. Only one strand of the double-stranded plasmid and cloned DNA is shown.

EXAMPLE OF A SEQUENCING REACTION

Tube	Reaction Products	
A	G-C-A-T-C-G-T-C C-G-T-**A**	G-C-A-T-C-G-T-C C-G-T-A-G-C-**A**
T	G-C-A-T-C-G-T-C C-G-**T**	
C	G-C-A-T-C-G-T-C **C** G-C-A-T-C-G-T-C	G-C-A-T-C-G-T-C C-G-T-A-G-**C** G-C-A-T-C-G-T-C
G	C-**G** G-C-A-T-C-G-T-C C-G-T-A-G-C-A-**G**	C-G-T-A-**G**

The Sanger sequencing reaction is set up in four separate tubes, each containing a different dideoxynucleotide (ddATP, ddTTP, ddCTP, and ddGTP). The reaction products are shown for each of the tubes: A (ddATP), T (ddTTP), C (ddCTP), and G (ddGTP). The template strand is GCATCGTC. Replication of the template begins after the primer binds to the primer site on the sequencing plasmid. The dideoxynucleotide terminating the reaction is shown in bold. The daughter strands, all of different lengths, are fractionated on a polyacrylamide gel.

complementary nucleotide at the beginning of the template; whereas the longest strand represents the complementary nucleotide at the end of the template (see table above). The reaction products, consisting of all the daughter strands, are fractionated on a polyacrylamide gel. Polyacrylamide serves the same function as agarose. It has the advantage of being a tougher material, essential for the large size of a typical sequencing gel. Some of the nucleotides included in the Sanger reaction are labeled with a radioactive isotope so the fractionated daughter strands can be visualized by drying the gel and then exposing it to X-ray film. Thus the Sanger method uses the natural process of replication to mark the position of each nucleotide in the DNA fragment so the sequence of the fragment can be determined.

A representation of a sequencing gel is shown in the accompanying figure. The sequence of the daughter strand is read beginning with the smallest fragment at the bottom of the gel and ending with the largest

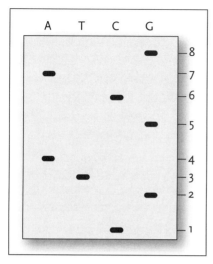

A representation of a sequencing gel. The reaction products (shown in table on page 105) run from the top to the bottom, with the smallest fragment migrating at the highest rate. The sequence is read beginning with the smallest fragment on the gel (band #1, in the "C" lane) and ending with the largest fragment at the top (band #8, in the "G" lane). The sequence is CGTAGCAG. The complementary sequence is GCATCGTC. This is the template strand indicated in the table.

fragment at the top. The sequence of the template strand (see table on page 105) is obtained simply by taking the complement of the sequence obtained from the gel (the daughter strand).

SOUTHERN AND NORTHERN BLOTTING

One of the most important techniques to be developed as part of recombinant technology is the transfer of nucleic acids from an agarose gel to nylon filter paper that can be hybridized to a labeled probe to detect specific genes. This procedure was introduced by the Scottish scientist E. M. Southern in 1975 for transferring DNA and is now known as Southern blotting. Since the DNA is transferred to filter paper, the detection stage is known as filter hybridization. In 1980 the procedure was modified to transfer RNA to nylon membranes for the study of gene expression and, in reference to the original, is called northern blotting.

Northern blotting is used to study the expression of specific genes and is usually performed on messenger RNA (mRNA). Typical experiments may wish to determine the expression of specific genes in normal, versus cancerous, tissue or tissues obtained from groups of different ages. The RNA is fractionated on an agarose gel and then transferred to a nylon membrane. The paper towels placed on top of the assembly pull the transfer buffer through the gel, eluting the RNA from the gel and trapping it on the membrane. The location of specific mRNA can be determined by hybridizing the membrane to a radiolabeled cDNA or

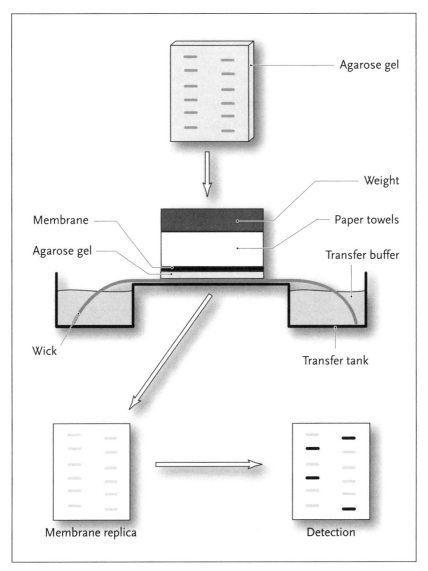

Agarose gel

Weight

Membrane

Paper towels

Agarose gel

Transfer buffer

Wick

Transfer tank

Membrane replica

Detection

Northern transfer and membrane hybridization. RNA is fractionated on an agarose gel and then placed face down on a paper wick in a transfer tank. The gel is overlaid with a piece of nylon membrane, paper towels, and weight. The paper towels draw the buffer through the gel and the membrane. The flow of buffer elutes the RNA from the gel, transferring it to the membrane. A radiolabeled cDNA probe is hybridized to the membrane to detect specific mRNA transcripts. Note that the thickness of the membrane is exaggerated for clarity.

genomic clone. The hybridization procedure involves placing the filter in a buffer solution containing a labeled probe. During a long incubation period, the probe binds to the target sequence immobilized on the membrane. A-T and G-C base pairing mediate the binding between the probe and target. The double-stranded molecule that is formed is a hybrid, being formed between the RNA target on the membrane and the DNA probe.

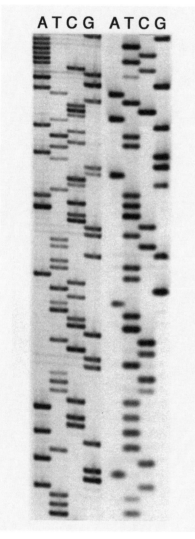

An autoradiogram of a portion of a DNA sequencing gel. A partial sequence (the first 20 bases) of the left set, beginning at the bottom of the "T" lane, is TTTAGGATGACCACTTTGGC. (Dr. Joseph P. Panno)

FLUORESCENT IN SITU HYBRIDIZATION (FISH)

Studying gene expression does not always depend on northern blots and filter hybridization. In the 1980s, scientists found that cDNA probes could be hybridized to DNA or mRNA in situ, that is, while located within cells or tissue sections fixed on a microscope slide. In this case, the probe is labeled with a fluorescent dye molecule, rather than a radioactive isotope. The samples are then examined and photographed under a fluorescent microscope. FISH is an extremely powerful variation on Southern and northern blots. This procedure gives precise information regarding the identity of a cell that expresses a specific gene, information that usually cannot be obtained with filter hybridization. Organs and tissues are generally composed of many different kinds of cells, which cannot be separated from each other using standard biochemical extraction procedures. Histological sections, however, show clearly the various cell types and when subjected to FISH analysis provide clear results as to which cells express specific genes. FISH is also used in clinical laboratories for the diagnosis of genetic abnormalities.

POLYMERASE CHAIN REACTION (PCR)

PCR is simply repetitive DNA replication over a limited, primer-defined region of a suitable template. The region defined by the primers is amplified to such an extent that it can be easily isolated for further study. The reaction exploits the fact that a DNA duplex in a low-salt buffer will melt (i.e., separate into two single strands) at 75°C but will reanneal (rehybridize) at 37°C. The reaction is initiated by melting the template, in the presence of primers and polymerase in a suitable buffer, cooling quickly to 37°C, and allowing sufficient time for the polymerase to replicate both strands of the template. The temperature is then increased to 75°C to melt the newly formed duplexes and then cooled to 37°C. At the lower temperature, more primer will anneal to initiate another round of replication. The heating-cooling cycle in repeated 20 to 30 times, after which the reaction products are fractionated on an agarose gel and photographed. The band containing the amplified fragment may be cut out of the gel and purified for further study. The DNA polymerase used in these reactions is isolated from thermophilic bacteria that can withstand temperatures of 70°C to 80°C. PCR applications are nearly limitless. It is used to amplify DNA from samples containing, at times, no more than a few cells. It can be used to screen libraries and to identify genes that are turned on or off during embryonic development or during cellular transformation.

The Human Genome Project

Sequencing the entire human genome is an idea that grew over a period of 20 years, beginning in the early 1980s. At that time, the DNA-sequencing method invented by the British biochemist Fred Sanger, then at the University of Cambridge, was just a few years old and had only been used to sequence viral or mitochondrial genomes (see chapter 8 for a description of sequencing methods). Indeed, one of the first genomes to be sequenced was that of bacteriophage G4, a virus that infects the bacterium *Escherichia coli (E. coli)*. The G4 genome consists of 5,577 nucleotide pairs (or base pairs, abbreviated bp) and was sequenced in Dr. Sanger's laboratory in 1979. By 1982 the Sanger protocol was used by others to sequence the genome of the animal virus SV40 (5,224 bp), the human mitochondrion (16,569 bp), and bacteriophage lambda (48,502 bp). Besides providing invaluable data, these projects demonstrated the feasibility of sequencing very large genomes.

The possibility of sequencing the entire human genome was first discussed at scientific meetings organized by the United States Department of Energy (DOE) between 1984 and 1986. A committee appointed by the U.S. National Research Council endorsed the idea in 1988 but recommended a broader program to include the sequencing of the genes of humans, bacteria, yeast, worms, flies, and mice. They also called for the establishment of research programs devoted to the ethical, legal, and social issues raised by human genome research. The program was formally launched in late 1990 as a consortium consisting of coordinated sequencing projects in the United States, Britain, France, Germany, Japan, and China. At about the same time, the Human Genome Organization (HUGO) was founded to provide a forum for international coordination of genomic research.

By 1995 the consortium had established a strategy, called hierarchical shotgun sequencing, which they applied to the human genome as well as to the other organisms mentioned. With this strategy, genomic DNA is cut into one-megabase (Mb) fragments (i.e., each fragment consists of 1 million bases) that are cloned into bacterial artificial chromosomes (BACs) to form a library of DNA fragments. The BAC fragments are partially characterized, then organized into an overlapping assembly called a contig. Clones are selected from the contigs for shotgun sequencing. That is, each shotgun clone is digested into small 1,000 bp fragments, sequenced, and then assembled into the final sequence with the aid of computers. Organizing the initial BAC fragments into contigs greatly simplifies the final assembly stage.

Sequencing of the human genome was divided into two stages. The first stage, completed in 2001, was a rough draft that covered about 80 percent of the genome with an estimated size of more than 3 billion bases (also expressed as 3 gigabases, or 3 Gb). The final draft, completed in April 2003, covers the entire genome and refines the data for areas of the genome that were difficult to sequence. It also filled in many gaps that occurred in the rough draft. The final draft of the human genome gives us a great deal of information that may be divided into three categories: gene content, gene origins, and gene organization.

GENE CONTENT

Analysis of the final draft has shown that the human genome consists of 3.2 Gb of DNA that encodes about 30,000 genes (estimates range between 25,000 to 32,000). The estimated number of genes is surprisingly low; many scientists had believed the human genome contained 100,000 genes. By comparison, the fruit fly has 13,338 genes and the simple roundworm, *Caenorhabditis elegans (C. elegans),* has 18,266. The genome data suggests that human complexity, as compared to the fruit fly or the worm, is not simply due to the absolute number of genes but involves the complexity of the proteins that are encoded by those genes. In general, human proteins tend to be much more complex than those of lower organisms. Data from the final draft and other sources provides a detailed overview of the functional profile of human cellular proteins.

GENE ORIGINS

Fully one half of human genes originated as transposable elements, also known as jumping genes. Equally surprising is the fact that 220 of our genes were obtained by horizontal transfer from bacteria, rather than ancestral, or vertical, inheritance. In other words, we obtained these genes directly from bacteria, probably during episodes of infection, in a kind of natural gene therapy or gene swapping. We know this to be the case because although these genes occur in bacteria, they are not present in yeast, fruit flies, or any other eukaryotes that have been tested.

The function of most of the horizontally transferred genes is unclear, although a few may code for basic metabolic enzymes. A notable exception is a gene that codes for an enzyme called mono-amine oxidase (MAO). Monoamines are neurotransmitters, such as dopamine, norepinephrine, and serotonin, which are needed for neural signaling in the human central nervous system. Monoamine oxidase plays a crucial role in the turnover of these neurotransmitters. How MAO, obtained from bacteria, could have developed such an important role in human physiology is a great mystery.

GENE ORGANIZATION

In prokaryotes, genes are simply arranged in tandem along the chromosome, with little if any DNA separating one gene from the other. Each gene is transcribed into messenger RNA (mRNA), which is translated into protein. Indeed, in prokaryotes, which have no nucleus, translation often begins even before transcription is complete. In eukaryotes, as we might expect, gene organization is more complex. Data from the genome project shows clearly that eukaryote genes are split into subunits, called exons, and that each exon is separated by a length of DNA, called an intron. A gene consisting of introns and exons is separated from other genes by long stretches of noncoding DNA called intervening sequences. Eukaryote genes are transcribed into a primary RNA molecule that includes exon and intron sequences. The primary transcript never leaves the nucleus and is never translated into protein. Nuclear enzymes remove the introns from the primary transcript, after which the exons are joined together to form the mature mRNA. Thus only the exons carry the necessary code to produce a protein.

The Belmont Report

On July 12, 1975, the American National Research Act was signed into law, thereby creating a national commission to protect human research subjects. This commission was charged with the task of identifying basic ethical principles that should govern the conduct of any research involving human subjects. In February 1976 the commission produced the Belmont Report (so named because the report was finalized at the Smithsonian Institution's Belmont Conference Center). The report began by defining three basic ethical principles that should be applied to research involving human subjects: respect for persons, beneficence, and justice.

RESPECT FOR PERSONS

Respect for persons demands that subjects enter into research voluntarily and with adequate information. This assumes the individuals are autonomous agents, that is, are competent to make up their own minds. However, there many instances where potential research subjects are not really autonomous: prisoners, patients in a mental institution, children, the elderly, and the infirm. All these people require special protection to ensure they are not being coerced or fooled into volunteering as research subjects. The subjects in the Tuskegee study were all poor, uneducated farm workers who were especially vulnerable to coercion.

BENEFICENCE

It is not enough to respect potential subjects' decisions and to protect them from harm, but in addition, it is necessary to do all that is possible to ensure their well-being. Beneficence is generally regarded as acts of kindness or charity, but the report insisted that in the case of research subjects, it should be an obligation. In this sense, it is the natural extension of the Hippocratic oath that all physicians are expected to adhere by: *I will give no deadly medicine to anyone if asked, nor suggest any such counsel.* In other words, physicians should do no harm, and those involved in biomedical research should never injure one person to benefit another.

JUSTICE

Those volunteering to be research subjects should, if at all possible, reap some of the benefits. This is a question of justice, in the sense of fairness of distribution. The exploitation of prisoners in Nazi concentration camps may have produced results that benefited the Nazis but certainly not the people they experimented on. The Tuskegee study used disadvantaged rural black men to study the untreated course of a disease that is by no means restricted to that population.

Guided by these three ethical principles, the report introduced the following requirements that all human research trials must adhere to:

informed consent, risk/benefit assessment, and fair selection of research subjects.

INFORMED CONSENT

All participants must provide informed consent, in writing. Moreover, steps must be taken to ensure the consent is in fact informed. This might involve an independent assessment of the individual's ability to understand the language on the consent form, as well as any instructions or explanations the investigators have given. Since the Gelsinger investigation, this process was amended to include a patient advocate, to be present at any meeting between the physicians and the prospective volunteers. This has the added advantage of ensuring that in a case where the patient is fully competent, the scientists do not give them misleading or inaccurate information or try to coerce them in any way.

RISK/BENEFIT ASSESSMENT

There is no point in having an ethical standard based on doing no harm, if there is no formalized method available for assessing the risk to patient. It is the risk that is paramount in a patient's mind. No matter how grand the possible benefits, few would volunteer if they thought they would die as a consequence. The only exception to this might be terminally ill patients who volunteer for a clinical trial, even though they know they are not likely survive it. Independent committees based on information supplied by the investigators monitor risk assessment. In general, risks should be reduced to those necessary to achieve the research objective. If there is significant risk, review committees are expected to demand a justification for it.

SELECTION OF SUBJECTS

The selection process must be fair. Low-risk, potentially beneficial research should not be offered to one segment of our society, while high-risk research is conducted on prisoners, low-income groups, or anyone in a disadvantaged social position.

CONCLUSIONS

The Belmont Report introduced, for the first time, the principle of informed consent. Backing this up is the recommendation that independent review committees ensure the ethical guidelines are being followed. In the United States, the FDA and NIH are responsible for enforcing the guidelines laid out by the Belmont Report. There are, in addition, local review committees, called institutional review boards, that must approve any experimentation using human subjects. The Belmont Report was inspired by the general public's anger over the Tuskegee study, and thus it is fitting that on May 16, 1997, the surviving members of the Tuskegee study were invited to the White House where the then president, Bill Clinton, issued a formal apology and reaffirmed the nation's commitment to rigorous ethical standards in biomedical research to ensure that such flagrant abuses of basic human rights would never happen again. No one would have believed at the time that further trouble was just around the corner.

The Gelsinger Investigation

In the fall of 1998, a gene therapy trial to treat a liver disease was begun at the University of Pennsylvania. The investigators recruited 18 patients, and the 18th patient, who happened to be 18 years of age, was Jesse Gelsinger. Gelsinger joined the trial on September 13, 1999. On the second day of his treatment, he lapsed into a coma, and was pronounced dead 24 hours later. Within days of Gelsinger's death, the National Institutes of Health (NIH) ordered a halt to all American gene therapy trials that were using a similar research protocol. The ban was to last a full year and was accompanied by an investigation that was not concluded until the fall of 2001.

The team leader of the clinical trial, Dr. James Wilson, reported Gelsinger's death immediately. A preliminary review was conducted from November 30, 1999, to January 19, 2000. The full review was to last for more than a year and covered every aspect of Dr. Wilson's protocol and the criteria used to admit patients to the trial. In January 2000, NIH released preliminary results of their investigation, which cited the principal investigators for failure to adhere to the clinical protocol and an apparent disregard for the safety of the study subjects. The report focused on four main points: failure to adhere to the stopping rules, failure to adhere to the principle of informed consent, failure to keep adequate records regarding vector lineage and titer, and changing the protocol without approval.

FAILURE TO ADHERE TO THE STOPPING RULES

The study was designed around several cohorts that were treated in tandem so that in the event of toxic reactions in one cohort treatment, the study could be terminated before other cohorts were treated. However, toxic reactions observed in five of the cohorts did not lead to termination of the trial before Gelsinger was treated. Many of the patients suffered harsher reactions to the treatment than expected, and this should have been sufficient reason to stop the trial. In addition, most of the toxic reactions experienced by the patients in this study were never reported to the FDA or NIH. In the months following the conclusion of the Gelsinger preliminary investigation, other investigations showed that failure to report toxic reactions was a common failure in many gene therapy trials. In one study, the patients experienced 691 serious side effects, and of these, only 39 were reported as required by the federal agencies.

FAILURE TO ADHERE TO THE PRINCIPLE OF INFORMED CONSENT

When a toxic response occurred in cohort 1, cohort 2 should have been informed of this response to give those patients the option of withdrawing from the study. This was not done. Moreover, the investigators discovered that none of the subjects were told about adverse affects on monkeys in the preclinical trial. One of the monkeys received the same virus used in the clinical trial, though at a higher dose, and within a week of being treated, it was euthanized because it developed the same clotting disorder that killed Gelsinger. Since the subjects were not told about this, the consent forms were ruled invalid. It was this charge that led to the call for a patient advocate in all future biomedical research trials, regardless of their nature.

FAILURE TO KEEP ADEQUATE RECORDS REGARDING VECTOR LINEAGE TITER

This was an especially damaging finding since it implied that the researchers gave Gelsinger more virus than they thought they had. The term *titer* refers to the number of vector particles in a given solution. Determining the titer is not straightforward, and if errors are made, the concentration may be off by increments of 10, rather than double or triple the amount expected. The possibility that Gelsinger was accidentally given a higher than stated dose is suggested by the fact that a woman in his cohort received a nearly identical dose (3.0×10^{13}) without signs of liver damage or multiorgan failure. As mentioned above, a monkey in a preclinical trial received a higher dose (17× greater) of the same virus and subsequently died of multiorgan failure. If there was an error made in calculating the dose for Gelsinger, it is possible he received an equivalent, fatal amount.

CHANGING THE PROTOCOL WITHOUT APPROVAL

The most serious infraction here had to do with the ammonia levels in the blood of prospective volunteers. As laid out in the original protocol, patients having more than 50 micromoles of ammonia per milliliter of blood were barred from volunteering because such a test result indicates severe liver damage. This was increased, sometime after the trial began, to 70 micromoles, without formal approval from the FDA. Gelsinger's ammonia level on the day he was treated was about 60 micromoles. If the original cutoff had been adhered to, he would have been excluded from the study. This is another indication of how important it is to adhere to the principle of informed consent and to the inclusion of an independent patient advocate.

Clinical Trials

Clinical trials are conducted in four phases and are always preceded by research conducted on experimental animals such as mice, rats, or monkeys. The format for preclinical research is informal; it is conducted in a variety of research labs around the world, with the results being published in scientific journals. Formal approval from a governmental regulatory body is not required.

PHASE I CLINICAL TRIAL

Pending the outcome of the preclinical research, investigators may apply for permission to try the experiments on human subjects. Applications in the United States are made to the Food and Drug Administration (FDA), the National Institutes of Health (NIH), and the Recombinant DNA Advisory Committee (RAC). RAC was set up by

NIH to monitor any research, including clinical trials, dealing with cloning, recombinant DNA, or gene therapy. Phase I trials are conducted on a small number of adult volunteers, usually between two and 20, who have given informed consent. That is, the investigators explain the procedure, the possible outcomes, and especially, the dangers associated with the procedure before the subjects sign a consent form. The purpose of the Phase I trial is to determine the overall effect the treatment has on humans. A treatment that works well in monkeys or mice may not work at all on humans. Similarly, a treatment that appears safe in lab animals may be toxic, even deadly, when given to humans. Since most clinical trials are testing a new drug of some kind, the first priority is to determine a safe dosage for humans. Consequently, subjects in the Phase I trial are given a range of doses, all of which, even the high dose, are less than the highest dose given to experimental animals. If the results from the Phase I trial are promising, the investigators may apply for permission to proceed to Phase II.

PHASE II CLINICAL TRIAL

Having established the general protocol, or procedure, the investigators now try to replicate the encouraging results from Phase I, but with a much larger number of subjects (100–300). Only with a large number of subjects is it possible to prove the treatment has an effect. In addition, dangerous side effects may have been missed in Phase I because of a small sample size. The results from Phase II will determine how safe the procedure is and whether it works or not. If the statistics show the treatment is effective, and toxicity is low, the investigators may apply for permission to proceed to Phase III.

PHASE III CLINICAL TRIAL

Based on Phase II results, the procedure may look very promising, but before it can be used as a routine treatment, it must be tested on thousands of patients at a variety of research centers. This is the expensive part of bringing a new drug or therapy to market, costing millions, sometimes billions, of dollars. It is for this reason that Phase III clinical trials invariably have the financial backing of large pharmaceutical or biotechnology companies. If the results of the Phase II trial are confirmed in Phase III, the FDA will approve the use of the drug for routine treatment. The use of the drug or treatment now passes into an informal Phase IV trial.

PHASE IV CLINICAL TRIAL

Even though the treatment has gained formal approval, its performance is monitored for very-long-term effects, sometimes stretching on for 10 to 20 years. In this way, the FDA retains the power to recall the drug long after it has become a part of standard medical procedure. It can happen that in the long term, the drug costs more than an alternative, in which case, health insurance providers may refuse to cover the cost of the treatment.

GLOSSARY

⚭

acetyl   A chemical group derived from acetic acid. Important in energy metabolism and for the modification of proteins.

acetylcholine   A neurotransmitter released at axonal terminals by cholinergic neurons. Found in the central and peripheral nervous system and released at the vertebrate neuromuscular junction.

acetyl-CoA   A water-soluble molecule, coenzyme A (CoA), that carries acetyl groups in cells.

acid   A substance that releases protons when dissolved in water. Carries a net negative charge.

actin filament   A protein filament formed by the polymerization of globular actin molecules. Forms the cytoskeleton of all eukaryotes and part of the contractile apparatus of skeletal muscle.

action potential   A self-propagating electrical impulse that occurs in the membranes of neurons, muscles, photoreceptors, and hair cells of the inner ear.

active transport   Movement of molecules across the cell membrane, utilizing the energy stored in ATP.

adenylate cyclase   A membrane-bound enzyme that catalyzes the conversion of ATP to cyclic AMP. An important component of cell-signaling pathways.

adherens junction   A cell junction in which the cytoplasmic face of the membrane is attached to actin filaments.

adipocyte   A fat cell.

adrenaline (epinephrine)   A hormone released by chromaffin cells in the adrenal gland. Prepares an animal for extreme activity, increases the heart rate and blood-sugar levels.

adult stem cells   Stem cells isolated from adult tissues, such as bone marrow or epithelium.

aerobic   Refers to a process that either requires oxygen or occurs in its presence.

allele   An alternate form of a gene. Diploid organisms have two alleles for each gene, located at the same locus (position) on homologous chromosomes.

allogeneic transplant   A patient receives a tissue or organ transplant from an unrelated individual.

alpha helix   A common folding pattern of proteins in which a linear sequence of amino acids twists into a right-handed helix stabilized by hydrogen bonds.

amino acid   An organic molecule containing amino and carboxyl groups that is a building block of protein.

aminoacyl-tRNA   An amino acid linked by its carboxyl group to a hydroxyl group on tRNA.

aminoacyl-tRNA synthetase   An enzyme that attaches the correct amino acid to a tRNA.

amino terminus   The end of a protein or polypeptide chain that carries a free amino group.

amphipathic   Having both hydrophilic and hydrophobic regions, as in a phospholipid.

anabolism   A collection of metabolic reactions in a cell whereby large molecules are made from smaller ones.

anaerobic   A cellular metabolism that does not depend on molecular oxygen.

anaphase   A mitotic stage in which the two sets of chromosomes move away from each other toward opposite and spindle poles.

anchoring junction   A cell junction that attaches cells to each other.

angiogenesis   Sprouting of new blood vessels from preexisting ones.

angstrom   A unit of length, equal to 10^{-10} meter or 0.1 nanometer (nm), that is used to measure molecules and atoms.

anterior   A position close to or at the head end of the body.

antibiotic   A substance made by bacteria, fungi, and plants that is toxic to microorganisms. Common examples are penicillin and streptomycin.

antibody   A protein made by B cells of the immune system in response to invading microbes.

anticodon   A sequence of three nucleotides in tRNA that is complementary to a messenger RNA codon.

antigen   A molecule that stimulates an immune response, leading to the formation of antibodies.

antigen-presenting cell   A cell of the immune system, such as a monocyte, that presents pieces of an invading microbe (the antigen) to lymphocytes.

antiparallel   The relative orientation of the two strands in a DNA double helix; the polarity of one strand is oriented in the opposite direction to the other.

antiporter   A membrane carrier protein that transports two different molecules across a membrane in opposite directions.

apoptosis   Regulated or programmed form of cell death that may be activated by the cell itself or by the immune system to force cells to commit suicide when they become infected with a virus.

asexual reproduction   The process of forming new individuals without gametes or the fertilization of an egg by a sperm. Individuals produced this way are identical to the parent and referred to as a clone.

aster   The star-shaped arrangement of microtubules that is characteristic of a mitotic or meiotic spindle.

ATP (adenosine triphosphate)   A nucleoside consisting of adenine, ribose, and three phosphate groups that is the main carrier of chemical energy in the cell.

ATPase   Any enzyme that catalyzes a biochemical reaction by extracting the necessary energy from ATP.

ATP synthase   A protein located in the inner membrane of the mitochondrion that catalyzes the formation of ATP from ADP and inorganic phosphate using the energy supplied by the electron transport chain.

autogeneic transplant   A patient receives a transplant of his or her own tissue.

autosome   Any chromosome other than a sex chromosome.

axon   A long extension of a neuron's cell body that transmits an electrical signal to other neurons.

axonal transport   The transport of organelles, such as Golgi vesicles, along an axon to the axonal terminus. Transport also flows from the terminus to the cell body.

bacteria   One of the most ancient forms of cellular life (the other is the Archaea). Bacteria are prokaryotes and some are known to cause disease.

bacterial artificial chromosome (BAC)   A cloning vector that accommodates DNA inserts of up to 1 million base pairs.

bacteriophage   A virus that infects bacteria. Bacteriophages were used to prove that DNA is the cell's genetic material and are now used as cloning vectors.

base   A substance that can accept a proton in solution. The purines and pyrimidines in DNA and RNA are organic bases and are often referred to simply as bases.

base pair   Two nucleotides in RNA or DNA that are held together by hydrogen bonds. Adenine bound to thymine or guanine bound to cytosine are examples of base pairs.

B cell (B lymphocyte)   A white blood cell that makes antibodies and is part of the adaptive immune response.

benign   Tumors that grow to a limited size and do not spread to other parts of the body.

beta sheet   Common structural motif in proteins in which different strands of the protein run alongside each other and are held together by hydrogen bonds.

biopsy   The removal of cells or tissues for examination under a microscope. When only a sample of tissue is removed, the procedure is called an incisional biopsy or core biopsy. When an entire lump or suspicious area is removed, the procedure is called an excisional biopsy. When a sample of tissue or fluid is removed with a needle, the procedure is called a needle biopsy or fine-needle aspiration.

biosphere   The world of living organisms.

bivalent   A duplicated chromosome paired with its homologous duplicated chromosome at the beginning of meiosis.

blastomere   A cell formed by the cleavage of a fertilized egg. Blastomeres are the totipotent cells of the early embryo.

blotting   A technique for transferring DNA (Southern blotting), RNA (northern blotting), or proteins (western blotting) from an agarose or polyacrylamide gel to a nylon membrane.

BRCA1 (breast cancer gene 1)   A gene on chromosome 17 that may be involved in regulating the cell cycle. A person who inherits an altered version of the BRCA1 gene has a higher risk of getting breast, ovarian, or prostate cancer.

BRCA2 (breast cancer gene 2)   A gene on chromosome 13 that, when mutated, increases the risk of getting breast, ovarian, or prostate cancer.

budding yeast   The common name for the baker's yeast *Saccharomyces cerevisiae,* a popular experimental organism that reproduces by budding off a parental cell.

cadherin   Belongs to a family of proteins that mediates cell-to-cell adhesion in animal tissues.

calorie   A unit of heat. One calorie is the amount of heat needed to raise the temperature of one gram of water by 1°C. Kilocalories (1,000 calories) are used to describe the energy content of foods.

capsid   The protein coat of a virus, formed by auto-assembly of one or more proteins into a geometrically symmetrical structure.

carbohydrate   A general class of compounds that includes sugars, containing carbon, hydrogen, and oxygen.

carboxyl group   A carbon atom attached to an oxygen and a hydroxyl group.

carboxyl terminus   The end of a protein containing a carboxyl group.

carcinogen   A compound or form of radiation that can cause cancer.

carcinogenesis   The formation of a cancer.

carcinoma   Cancer of the epithelium, representing the majority of human cancers.

cardiac muscle   Muscle of the heart. Composed of myocytes that are linked together in a communication network based on free passage of small molecules through gap junctions.

caspase   A protease involved in the initiation of apoptosis.

catabolism   Enzyme-regulated breakdown of large molecules for the extraction of chemical-bond energy. Intermediate products are called catabolites.

catalyst   A substance that lowers the activation energy of a reaction.

CD28   Cell-surface protein located in T cell membranes, necessary for the activation of T cells by foreign antigens.

cDNA (complementary DNA)   DNA that is synthesized from mRNA, thus containing the complementary sequence. cDNA contains coding sequence but not the regulatory sequences that are present in the genome. Labeled probes are made from cDNA for the study of gene expression.

cell adhesion molecule (CAM) A cell surface protein that is used to connect cells to each other.

cell body The main part of a cell containing the nucleus, Golgi complex, and endoplasmic reticulum. Used in reference to neurons that have long processes (dendrites and axons) extending some distance from the nucleus and cytoplasmic machinery.

cell coat See **glycocalyx**.

cell-cycle control system A team of regulatory proteins that governs progression through the cell cycle.

cell-division-cycle gene (*cdc* gene) A gene that controls a specific step in the cell cycle.

cell fate The final differentiated state that a pluripotent embryonic cell is expected to attain.

cell-medicated immune response Activation of specific cells to launch an immune response against an invading microbe.

cell nuclear replacement Animal-cloning technique whereby a somatic cell nucleus is transferred to an enucleated oocyte. Synonomous with somatic-cell nuclear transfer.

central nervous system (CNS) That part of a nervous system that analyzes signals from the body and the environment. In animals, the CNS includes the brain and spinal cord.

centriole A cylindrical array of microtubules that is found at the center of a centrosome in animal cells.

centromere A region of a mitotic chromosome that holds sister chromatids together. Microtubules of the spindle fiber connect to an area of the centromere called the kinetochore.

centrosome Organizes the mitotic spindle and the spindle poles. In most animal cells it contains a pair of centrioles.

chiasma (plural: chiasmata) An X-shaped connection between homologous chromosomes that occurs during meiosis I, representing a site of crossing-over, or genetic exchange between the two chromosomes.

chromatid A duplicate chromosome that is still connected to the original at the centromere. The identical pair are called sister chromatids.

chromatin A complex of DNA and proteins (histones and nonhistones) that forms each chromosome and is found in the nucleus of all eukaryotes. Decondensed and threadlike during interphase.

chromatin condensation Compaction of different regions of interphase chromosomes that is mediated by the histones.

chromosome One long molecule of DNA that contains the organism's genes. In prokaryotes, the chromosome is circular and naked; in eukaryotes, it is linear and complexed with histone and nonhistone proteins.

chromosome condensation Compaction of entire chromosomes in preparation for cell division.

clinical breast exam An exam of the breast performed by a physician to check for lumps or other changes.

cyclic adenosine monophosphate (cAMP) A second messenger in a cell-signaling pathway that is produced from ATP by the enzyme adenylate cyclase.

cyclin A protein that activates protein kinases (cyclin-dependent protein kinases, or Cdk) that control progression from one state of the cell cycle to another.

cytochemistry The study of the intracellular distribution of chemicals.

cytochrome Colored, iron-containing protein that is part of the electron transport chain.

cytotoxic T cell A T lymphocyte that kills infected body cells.

dendrite An extension of a nerve cell that receives signals from other neurons.

dexrazoxane A drug used to protect the heart from the toxic effects of anthracycline drugs such as doxorubicin. It belongs to the family of drugs called chemoprotective agents.

dideoxy sequencing A method for sequencing DNA that employs dideoxyribose nucleotides.

diploid A genetic term meaning two sets of homologous chromosomes, one set from the mother and the other from the father. Thus diploid organisms have two versions (alleles) of each gene in the genome.

DNA (deoxyribonucleic acid) A long polymer formed by linking four different kinds of nucleotides together like beads on a string. The sequence of nucleotides is used to encode an organism's genes.

DNA helicase   An enzyme that separates and unwinds the two DNA strands in preparation for replication or transcription.

DNA library   A collection of DNA fragments that are cloned into plasmids or viral genomes.

DNA ligase   An enzyme that joins two DNA strands together to make a continuous DNA molecule.

DNA microarray   A technique for studying the simultaneous expression of a very large number of genes.

DNA polymerase   An enzyme that synthesizes DNA using one strand as a template.

DNA primase   An enzyme that synthesizes a short strand of RNA that serves as a primer for DNA replication.

dorsal   The backside of an animal. Also refers to the upper surface of anatomical structures, such as arms or wings.

dorsoventral   The body axis running from the backside to the frontside or the upperside to the underside of a structure.

double helix   The three-dimensional structure of DNA in which the two strands twist around each other to form a spiral.

doxorubicin   An anticancer drug that belongs to a family of antitumor antibiotics.

Drosophila melanogaster   Small species of fly, commonly called a fruit fly, that is used as an experimental organism in genetics, embryology, and gerontology.

ductal carcinoma in situ (DCIS)   Abnormal cells that involve only the lining of a breast duct. The cells have not spread outside the duct to other tissues in the breast. Also called intraductal carcinoma.

dynein   A motor protein that is involved in chromosome movements during cell division.

dysplasia   Disordered growth of cells in a tissue or organ, often leading to the development of cancer.

ectoderm   An embryonic tissue that is the precursor of the epidermis and the nervous system.

electrochemical gradient   A differential concentration of an ion or molecule across the cell membrane that serves as a source of potential energy and may polarize the cell electrically.

electron microscope   A microscope that uses electrons to produce a high-resolution image of the cell.

embryogensis   The development of an embryo from a fertilized egg.

embryonic stem cell (ES cell)   A pluripotent cell derived from the inner cell mass (the cells that give rise to the embryo instead of the placenta) of a mammalian embryo.

endocrine cell   A cell that is specialized for the production and release of hormones. Such cells make up hormone-producing tissue such as the pituitary gland or gonads.

endocytosis   Cellular uptake of material from the environment by invagination of the cell membrane to form a vesicle called an endosome. The endosome's contents are made available to the cell after it fuses with a lysosome.

endoderm   An embryonic tissue layer that gives rise to the gut.

endoplasmic reticulum (ER)   Membrane-bounded chambers that are used to modify newly synthesized proteins with the addition of sugar molecules (glycosylation). When finished, the glycosylated proteins are sent to the Golgi apparatus in exocytotic vesicles.

endothelial cell   A cell that forms the endothelium, a thin sheet of cells lining the inner surface of all blood vessels.

enhancer   A DNA regulatory sequence that provides a binding site for transcription factors capable of increasing the rate of transcription for a specific gene. Often located thousands of base pairs away from the gene it regulates.

enveloped virus   A virus containing a capsid that is surrounded by a lipid bilayer originally obtained from the membrane of a previously infected cell.

enzyme   A protein or RNA that catalyzes a specific chemical reaction.

epidermis   The epithelial layer, or skin, that covers the outer surface of the body.

ER signal sequence   The amino terminal sequence that directs proteins to enter the endoplasmic reticulum (ER). This sequence is removed once the protein enters the ER.

erythrocyte   A red blood cell that contains the oxygen-carrying pigment hemoglobin used to deliver oxygen to cells in the body.

***Escherichia coli* (*E. coli*)**   Rod shape, gram negative bacterium that inhabits the intestinal tract of most animals and is used as an experimental organism by geneticists and biomedical researchers.

euchromatin Lightly staining portion of interphase chromatin, in contrast to the darkly staining heterochromatin (condensed chromatin). Euchromatin contains most, if not all, of the active genes.

eukaryote (eucaryote) A cell containing a nucleus and many membrane-bounded organelles. All life-forms, except bacteria and viruses, are composed of eukaryote cells.

exocytosis The process by which molecules are secreted from a cell. Molecules to be secreted are located in Golgi-derived vesicles that fuse with the inner surface of the cell membrane, depositing the contents into the intercellular space.

exon Coding region of a eukaryote gene that is represented in messenger RNA, and thus directs the synthesis of a specific protein.

expression studies Examination of the type and quantity of mRNA or protein that is produced by cells, tissues, or organs.

fat A lipid material, consisting of triglycerides (fatty acids bound to glycerol), that is stored adipocytes as an energy reserve.

fatty acid A compound that has a carboxylic acid attached to a long hydrocarbon chain. A major source of cellular energy and a component of phospholipids.

filter hybridization The detection of specific DNA or RNA molecules, fixed on a nylon filter, by incubating the filter with a labeled probe that hybridizes to the target sequence.

fertilization The fusion of haploid male and female gametes to form a diploid zygote.

fibroblast The cell type that, by secreting an extracellular matrix, gives rise to the connective tissue of the body.

fixative A chemical that is used to preserve cells and tissues. Common examples are formaldehyde, methanol, and acetic acid.

flagellum (plural: flagella) Whiplike structure found in prokaryotes and eukaryotes that are used to propel cells through water.

fluorescein Fluorescent dye that produces a green light when illuminated with ultraviolet or blue light.

fluorescent dye A dye that absorbs UV or blue light and emits light of a longer wavelength, usually as green or red light.

fluorescent microscope A microscope that is equipped with special filters and a beam splitter for the examination of tissues and cells stained with a fluorescent dye.

follicle cell   Cells that surround and help feed a developing oocyte.

G₀   G "zero" refers to a phase of the cell cycle. State of withdrawal from the cycle as the cell enters a resting or quiescent stage. Occurs in differentiated body cells as well as developing oocytes.

G₁   Gap 1 refers to the phase of the cell cycle that occurs just after mitosis and before the next round of DNA synthesis.

G₂   Gap 2 refers to the phase of the cell cycle that follows DNA replication and precedes mitosis.

gap junction   A communication channel in the membranes of adjacent cells that allows free passage of ions and small molecules.

gastrulation   An embryological event in which a spherical embryo is converted into an elongated structure with a head end, a tail end, and a gut (gastrula).

gene   A region of the DNA that specifies a specific protein or RNA molecule that is handed down from one generation to the next. This region includes both the coding, noncoding, and regulatory sequences.

gene regulatory protein   Any protein that binds to DNA and thereby affects the expression of a specific gene.

gene repressor protein   A protein that binds to DNA and blocks transcription of a specific gene.

gene therapy   A method for treating disease whereby a defective gene, causing the disease, is either repaired, replaced, or supplemented with a functional copy.

genetic code   A set of rules that assigns a specific DNA or RNA triplet, consisting of a three-base sequence, to a specific amino acid.

genome   All of the genes that belong to a cell or an organism.

genomic library   A collection of DNA fragments, obtained by digesting genomic DNA with a restriction enzyme, that are cloned into plasmid or viral vectors.

genomics   The study of DNA sequences and their role in the function and structure of an organism.

genotype   The genetic composition of a cell or organism.

germ cell   Cells that develop into gametes, either sperm or oocytes.

glucose   Six-carbon monosaccharide (sugar) that is the principal source of energy for many cells and organisms. Stored as glycogen in animal cells and as starch in plants. Wood is an elaborate polymer of glucose and other sugars.

glycerol   A three-carbon alcohol that is an important component of phospholipids.

glycocalyx   A molecular "forest," consisting of glycosylated proteins and lipids, that covers the surface of every cell. The glycoproteins and glycolipids, carried to the cell membrane by Golgi-derived vesicles, have many functions, including the formation of ion channels, cell-signaling receptors and transporters.

glycogen   A polymer of glucose used to store energy in an animal cell.

glycolysis   The degradation of glucose with production of ATP.

glycoprotein   Any protein that has a chain of glucose molecules (oligosaccharide) attached to some of the amino acid residues.

glycosylation   The process of adding one or more sugar molecules to proteins or lipids.

glycosyl transferase   An enzyme in the Golgi complex that adds glucose to proteins.

Golgi complex (Golgi apparatus)   Membrane-bounded organelle in eukaryote cells that receives glycoproteins from the ER, which are modified and sorted before being sent to their final destination. The Golgi complex is also the source of glycolipids that are destined for the cell membrane. The glycoproteins and glycolipids leave the Golgi by exocytosis. This organelle is named after the Italian histologist Camillo Golgi, who discovered it in 1898.

granulocyte   A type of white blood cell that includes the neutrophils, basophils, and eosinophils.

growth factor   A small protein (polypeptide) that can stimulate cells to grow and proliferate.

haploid   Having only one set of chromosomes. A condition that is typical in gametes, such as sperm and eggs.

HeLa cell   A tumor-derived cell line, originally isolated from a cancer patient in 1951. Currently used by many laboratories to study the cell biology of cancer and carcinogenesis.

helix-loop-helix   A structural motif common to a group of gene regulatory proteins.

helper T cell   A type of T lymphocyte that helps stimulate B cells to make antibodies directed against a specific microbe or antigen.

hemoglobin   An iron-containing protein complex, located in red blood cells that picks up oxygen in the lungs and carries it to other tissues and cells of the body.

hemopoiesis   Production of blood cells, occurring primarily in the bone marrow.

hepatocyte   A liver cell.

heterochromatin   A region of a chromosome that is highly condensed and transcriptionally inactive.

histochemistry   The study of chemical differentiation of tissues.

histology   The study of tissues.

histone   Small nuclear proteins, rich in the amino acids arginine and lysine, that form the nucleosome in eukaryote nuclei, a beadlike structure that is a major component of chromatin.

HIV   The human immunodeficiency virus that is responsible for AIDS.

homolog   One of two or more genes that have a similar sequence and are descended from a common ancestor gene.

homologous   Organs or molecules that are similar in structure because they have descended from a common ancestor. Used primarily in reference to DNA and protein sequences.

homologous chromosomes   Two copies of the same chromosome, one inherited from the mother and the other from the father.

hormone   A signaling molecule, produced and secreted by endocrine glands. Usually released into general circulation for coordination of an animal's physiology.

housekeeping gene   A gene that codes for a protein that is needed by all cells, regardless of the cell's specialization. Genes encoding enzymes involved in glycolysis and the Krebs cycle are common examples.

hybridization   A term used in molecular biology (recombinant DNA technology) meaning the formation of a double-stranded nucleic acid through complementary base-pairing. A property that is exploited in filter hybridization, a procedure that is used to screen gene libraries and to study gene structure and expression.

hydrophilic   A polar compound that mixes readily with water.

hydrophobic   A nonpolar molecule that dissolves in fat and lipid solutions but not in water.

hydroxyl group (-OH) Chemical group consisting of oxygen and hydrogen that is a prominent part of alcohol.

image analysis A computerized method for extracting information from digitized microscopic images of cells or cell organelles.

immunofluorescence Detection of a specific cellular protein with the aid of a fluorescent dye that is coupled to an antibody.

immunoglobulin (Ig) An antibody made by B cells as part of the adaptive immune response.

incontinence Inability to control the flow of urine from the bladder (urinary incontinence) or the escape of stool from the rectum (fecal incontinence).

in situ hybridization A method for studying gene expression, whereby a labeled cDNA or RNA probe hybridizes to a specific mRNA in intact cells or tissues. The procedure is usually carried out on tissue sections or smears of individual cells.

insulin Polypeptide hormone secreted by β (beta) cells in the vertebrate pancreas. Production of this hormone is regulated directly by the amount of glucose that is in the blood.

interleukin A small protein hormone, secreted by lymphocytes, to activate and coordinate the adaptive immune response.

interphase The period between each cell division, which includes the G_1, S, and G_2 phases of the cell cycle.

intron A section of a eukaryote gene that is non-coding. It is transcribed, but does not appear in the mature mRNA.

in vitro Refers to cells growing in culture, or a biochemical reaction occurring in a test tube (Latin for "in glass").

in vivo A biochemical reaction, or a process, occurring in living cells or a living organism (Latin for "in life").

ion An atom that has gained or lost electrons, thus acquiring a charge. Common examples are Na^+ and Ca^{++} ions.

ion channel A transmembrane channel that allows ions to diffuse across the membrane and down their electrochemical gradient.

Jak-STAT signaling pathway One of several cell-signaling pathways that activates gene expression. The pathway is activated through cell-surface receptors and cytoplasmic Janus kinases (Jaks), and signal transducers and activators of transcription (STATs).

karyotype   A pictorial catalog of a cell's chromosomes, showing their number, size, shape, and overall banding pattern.

keratin   Proteins produced by specialized epithelial cells called keratinocytes. Keratin is found in hair, fingernails, and feathers.

kinesin   A motor protein that uses energy obtained from the hydrolysis of ATP to move along a microtubule.

kinetochore   A complex of proteins that forms around the centromere of mitotic or meiotic chromosomes, providing an attachment site for microtubules. The other end of each microtubule is attached to a chromosome.

Krebs cycle (citric acid cycle)   The central metabolic pathway in all eukaryotes and aerobic prokaryotes, discovered by the German chemist Hans Krebs in 1937. The cycle oxidizes acetyl groups derived from food molecules. The end products are CO_2, H_2O, and high-energy electrons, which pass via NADH and FADH2 to the respiratory chain. In eukaryotes, the Krebs cycle is located in the mitochondria.

labeling reaction   The addition of a radioactive atom or fluorescent dye to DNA or RNA for use as a probe in filter hybridization.

lagging strand   One of the two newly synthesized DNA strands at a replication fork. The lagging strand is synthesized discontinuously, and therefore, its completion lags behind the second, or leading, strand.

lambda bacteriophage   A viral parasite that infects bacteria. Widely used as a DNA cloning vector.

leading strand   One of the two newly synthesized DNA strands at a replication fork. The leading strand is made by continuous synthesis in the 5' to 3' direction.

leucine zipper   A structural motif of DNA binding proteins, in which two identical proteins are joined together at regularly spaced leucine residues, much like a zipper, to form a dimer.

leukemia   Cancer of white blood cells.

lipid bilayer   Two closely aligned sheets of phospholipids that form the core structure of all cell membranes. The two layers are aligned such that the hydrophobic tails are interior, while the hydrophilic head groups are exterior on both surfaces.

liposome   An artificial lipid bilayer vesicle used in membrane studies and as an artificial gene therapy vector.

locus   A term from genetics that refers to the position of a gene along a chromosome. Different alleles of the same gene occupy the same locus.

long-term potentiation (LTP)   A physical remodeling of synaptic junctions that receive continuous stimulation.

lymphocyte   A type of white blood cell that is involved in the adaptive immune response. There are two kinds of lymphocytes: T lymphocytes and B lymphocytes. T lymphocytes (T cells) mature in the thymus and attack invading microbes directly. B lymphocytes (B cells) mature in the bone marrow and make antibodies that are designed to immobilize or destroy specific microbes or antigens.

lysis   The rupture of the cell membrane followed by death of the cell.

lysosome   Membrane-bounded organelle of eukaryotes that contains powerful digestive enzymes.

macromolecule   A very large molecule that is built from smaller molecular subunits. Common examples are DNA, proteins, and polysaccharides.

magnetic resonance imaging (MRI)   A procedure in which radio waves and a powerful magnet linked to a computer are used to create detailed pictures of areas inside the body. These pictures can show the difference between normal and diseased tissue. MRI makes better images of organs and soft tissue than other scanning techniques, such as CT or X-ray. MRI is especially useful for imaging the brain, spine, the soft tissue of joints, and the inside of bones. Also called nuclear magnetic resonance imaging.

major histocompatibility complex   Vertebrate genes that code for a large family of cell-surface glycoproteins that bind foreign antigens and present them to T cells to induce an immune response.

malignant   Refers to the functional status of a cancer cell that grows aggressively and is able to metastasize, or colonize, other areas of the body.

mammography   The use of X-rays to create a picture of the breast.

MAP-kinase (mitogen-activated protein kinase)   A protein kinase that is part of a cell-proliferation-inducing signaling pathway.

M-cyclin   A eukaryote enzyme that regulates mitosis.

meiosis   A special form of cell division by which haploid gametes are produced. This is accomplished with two rounds of cell division but only one round of DNA replication.

melanocyte   A skin cell that produces the pigment melanin.

membrane   The lipid bilayer, and the associated glycocalyx, that surrounds and encloses all cells.

membrane channel   A protein complex that forms a pore or channel through the membrane for the free passage of ions and small molecules.

membrane potential   A buildup of charged ions on one side of the cell membrane establishes an electrochemical gradient that is measured in millivolts (mV). An important characteristic of neurons as it provides the electric current, when ion channels open, that enable these cells to communicate with each other.

mesoderm   An embryonic germ layer that gives rise to muscle, connective tissue, bones, and many internal organs.

messenger RNA (mRNA)   An RNA transcribed from a gene that is used as the gene template by the ribosomes, and other components of the translation machinery, to synthesize a protein.

metabolism   The sum total of the chemical processes that occur in living cells.

metaphase   The stage of mitosis at which the chromosomes are attached to the spindle but have not begun to move apart.

metaphase plate   Refers to the imaginary plane established by the chromosomes as they line up at right angles to the spindle poles.

metaplasia   A change in the pattern of cellular behavior that often precedes the development of cancer.

metastasis   Spread of cancer cells from the site of the original tumor to other parts of the body.

methyl group (-CH$_3$)   Hydrophobic chemical group derived from methane. Occurs at the end of a fatty acid.

micrograph   Photograph taken through a light, or electron, microscope.

micrometer (μm or micron)   Equal to 10^{-6} meters.

microtubule   A fine cylindrical tube made of the protein tubulin, forming a major component of the eukaryote cytoskeleton.

millimeter (mm)   Equal to 10^{-3} meters.

mitochondrion (plural: mitochondria)   Eukaryote organelle, formerly free-living, that produces most of the cell's ATP.

mitogen   A hormone or signaling molecule that stimulates cells to grow and divide.

mitosis   Division of a eukaryotic nucleus. From the Greek *mitos,* meaning "a thread," in reference to the threadlike appearance of interphase chromosomes.

mitotic chromosome   Highly condensed duplicated chromosomes held together by the centromere. Each member of the pair is referred to as a sister chromatid.

mitotic spindle   Array of microtubules, fanning out from the polar centrioles and connecting to each of the chromosomes.

molecule   Two or more atoms linked together by covalent bonds.

monoclonal antibody   An antibody produced from a B cell–derived clonal line. Since all of the cells are clones of the original B cell, the antibodies produced are identical.

monocyte   A type of white blood cell that is involved in the immune response.

motif   An element of structure or pattern that may be a recurring domain in a variety of proteins.

M phase   The period of the cell cycle (mitosis or meiosis) when the chromosomes separate and migrate to the opposite poles of the spindle.

multipass transmembrane protein   A membrane protein that passes back and forth across the lipid bilayer.

mutant   A genetic variation within a population.

mutation   A heritable change in the nucleotide sequence of a chromosome.

myelin sheath   Insulation applied to the axons of neurons. The sheath is produced by oligodendrocytes in the central nervous system and by Schwann cells in the peripheral nervous system.

myeloid cell   White blood cells other than lymphocytes.

myoblast   Muscle precursor cell. Many myoblasts fuse into a syncytium, containing many nuclei, to form a single muscle cell.

myocyte   A muscle cell.

NAD (nicotine adenine dinucleotide)   Accepts a hydride ion (H^-), produced by the Krebs cycle, forming NADH, the main carrier of electrons for oxidative phosphorylation.

NADH dehydrogenase   Removes electrons from NADH and passes them down the electron transport chain.

nanometer (nm)   Equal to 10^{-9} meters or 10^{-3} microns.

natural killer cell (NK cell)   A lymphocyte that kills virus-infected cells in the body. It also kills foreign cells associated with a tissue or organ transplant.

neuromuscular junction   A special form of synapse between a motor neuron and a skeletal muscle cell.

neuron   A cell specially adapted for communication that forms the nervous system of all animals.

neurotransmitter   A chemical released by neurons at a synapse that transmits a signal to another neuron.

non-small-cell lung cancer   A group of lung cancers that includes squamous cell carcinoma, adenocarcinoma, and large cell carcinoma. The small cells are endocrine cells.

northern blotting   A technique for the study of gene expression. Messenger RNA (mRNA) is fractionated on an agarose gel and then transferred to a piece of nylon filter paper (or membrane). A specific mRNA is detected by hybridization with a labeled DNA or RNA probe. The original blotting technique invented by E. M. Southern inspired the name.

nuclear envelope   The double membrane (two lipid bilayers) enclosing the cell nucleus.

nuclear localization signal (NLS)   A short amino acid sequence located on proteins that are destined for the cell nucleus after they are translated in the cytoplasm.

nucleic acid   DNA or RNA, a macromolecule consisting of a chain of nucleotides.

nucleolar organizer   Region of a chromosome containing a cluster of ribosomal RNA genes that gives rise to the nucleolus.

nucleolus   A structure in the nucleus where ribosomal RNA is transcribed and ribosomal subunits are assembled.

nucleoside   A purine or pyrimidine linked to a ribose or deoxyribose sugar.

nucleosome   A beadlike structure, consisting of histone proteins.

nucleotide   A nucleoside containing one or more phosphate groups linked to the 5' carbon of the ribose sugar. DNA and RNA are nucleotide polymers.

nucleus Eukaryote cell organelle that contains the DNA genome on one or more chromosomes.

oligodendrocyte A myelinating glia cell of the vertebrate central nervous system.

oligo labeling A method for incorporating labeled nucleotides into a short piece of DNA or RNA. Also known as the random-primer labeling method.

oligomer A short polymer, usually consisting of amino acids (oligopeptides), sugars (oligosaccharides), or nucleotides (oligonucleotides). Taken from the Greek word *oligos,* meaning "few" or "little."

oncogene A mutant form of a normal cellular gene, known as a proto-oncogene, that can transform a cell to a cancerous phenotype.

oocyte A female gamete or egg cell.

operator A region of a prokaryote chromosome that controls the expression of adjacent genes.

operon Two or more prokaryote genes that are transcribed into a single mRNA.

organelle A membrane-bounded structure, occurring in eukaryote cells, that has a specialized function. Examples are the nucleus, Golgi complex, and endoplasmic reticulum.

osmosis The movement of solvent across a semipermeable membrane that separates a solution with a high concentration of solutes from one with a low concentration of solutes. The membrane must be permeable to the solvent but not to the solutes. In the context of cellular osmosis, the solvent is always water, the solutes are ions and molecules, and the membrane is the cell membrane.

osteoblast Cells that form bones.

ovulation Rupture of a mature follicle with subsequent release of a mature oocyte from the ovary.

oxidative phosphorylation Generation of high-energy electrons from food molecules that are used to power the synthesis of ATP from ADP and inorganic phosphate. The electrons are eventually transferred to oxygen to complete the process. Occurs in bacteria and mitochondria.

p53 A tumor-suppressor gene that is mutated in about half of all human cancers. The normal function of the *p53* protein is to block passage through the cell cycle when DNA damage is detected.

parthenogenesis   A natural form of animal cloning whereby an individual is produced without the formation of haploid gametes and the fertilization of an egg.

pathogen   An organism that causes disease.

PCR (polymerase chain reaction)   A method for amplifying specific regions of DNA by temperature cycling a reaction mixture containing the template, a heat-stable DNA polymerase, and replication primers.

peptide bond   The chemical bond that links amino acids together to form a protein.

pH   Measures the acidity of a solution as a negative logarithmic function (p) of H^+ concentration (H). Thus a pH of 2.0 (10^{-2} molar H^+) is acidic, whereas a pH of 8.0 (10^{-8} molar H^+) is basic.

phagocyte   A cell that engulfs other cells or debris by phagocytosis.

phagocytosis   A process whereby cells engulf other cells or organic material by endocytosis. A common practice among protozoans and cells of the vertebrate immune system. (Derived from the Greek word *phagein*, "to eat.")

phenotype   Physical characteristics of a cell or organism.

phospholipid   The kind of lipid molecule used to construct cell membranes. Composed of a hydrophilic head-group, phosphate, glycerol, and two hydrophobic fatty acid tails.

phosphorylation   A chemical reaction in which a phosphate is covalently bonded to another molecule.

photoreceptor   A molecule or cell that responds to light.

photosynthesis   A biochemical process in which plants, algae, and certain bacteria use energy obtained from sunlight to synthesize macromolecules from CO_2 and H_2O.

phylogeny   The evolutionary history of an organism, or group of organisms, often represented diagrammatically as a phylogenetic tree.

pinocytosis   A form of endocytosis whereby fluid is brought into the cell from the environment.

placebo   An inactive substance that looks the same, and is administered in the same way, as a drug in a clinical trial.

plasmid   A minichromosome, often carrying antibiotic-resistant genes, that occurs naturally among prokaryotes. Used extensively as a DNA cloning vector.

platelet A cell fragment, derived from megakaryocytes and lacking a nucleus, that is present in the bloodstream and is involved in blood coagulation.

ploidy The total number of chromosomes (n) that a cell has. Ploidy is also measured as the amount of DNA (C) in a given cell relative to a haploid nucleus of the same organism. Most organisms are diploid, having two sets of chromosomes, one from each parent, but there is great variation among plants and animals. The silk gland of the moth *Bombyx mori*, for example, has cells that are extremely polyploid, reaching values of 100,000C. Flowers are often highly polyploid, and vertebrate hepatocytes may be 16C.

point mutation A change in DNA, particularly in a region containing a gene, that alters a single nucleotide.

polyploid Possessing more than two sets of homologous chromosomes.

portal system A system of liver vessels that carries liver enzymes directly to the digestive tract.

probe Usually a fragment of a cloned DNA molecule that is labeled with a radioisotope or fluorescent dye and used to detect specific DNA or RNA molecules on Southern or northern blots.

promoter A DNA sequence to which RNA polymerase binds to initiate gene transcription.

prophase The first stage of mitosis. The chromosomes are duplicated and beginning to condense but are attached to the spindle.

protein A major constituent of cells and organisms. Proteins, made by linking amino acids together, are used for structural purposes and regulate many biochemical reactions in their alternative role as enzymes. Proteins range in size from just a few amino acids to more than 200.

protein glycosylation The addition of sugar molecules to a protein.

proto-oncogene A normal gene that can be converted to a cancer-causing gene (oncogene) by a point mutation or through inappropriate expression.

protozoa Free-living, single-cell eukaryotes that feed on bacteria and other microorganisms. Common examples are *Paramecium* and *Amoeba*. Parasitic forms are also known that inhabit the digestive and urogenital tract of many animals, including humans.

purine A nitrogen-containing compound that is found in RNA and DNA. Two examples are adenine and guanine.

pyrimidine A nitrogen-containing compound found in RNA and DNA. Examples are cytosine, thymine, and uracil (RNA only).

radioactive isotope An atom with an unstable nucleus that emits radiation as it decays.

randomized clinical trial A study in which the participants are assigned by chance to separate groups that compare different treatments; neither the researchers nor the participants can choose which group. Using chance to assign people to groups means that the groups will be similar and that the treatments they receive can be compared objectively. At the time of the trial, it is not known which treatment is best.

reagent A chemical solution designed for a specific biochemical or histochemical procedure.

recombinant DNA A DNA molecule that has been formed by joining two or more fragments from different sources.

regulatory sequence A DNA sequence to which proteins bind that regulate the assembly of the transcriptional machinery.

replication bubble Local dissociation of the DNA double helix in preparation for replication. Each bubble contains two replication forks.

replication fork The Y-shaped region of a replicating chromosome. Associated with replication bubbles.

replication origin (origin of replication, ORI) The location at which DNA replication begins.

respiratory chain (electron transport chain) A collection of iron- and copper-containing proteins, located in the inner mitochondrion membrane, that utilize the energy of electrons traveling down the chain to synthesize ATP.

restriction enzyme An enzyme that cuts DNA at specific sites.

restriction map The size and number of DNA fragments obtained after digesting with one or more restriction enzymes.

retrovirus A virus that converts its RNA genome to DNA once it has infected a cell.

reverse transcriptase An RNA-dependent DNA polymerase. This enzyme synthesizes DNA by using RNA as a template, the reverse of the usual flow of genetic information from DNA to RNA.

ribosomal RNA (rRNA) RNA that is part of the ribosome and serves both a structural and functional role, possibly by catalyzing some of the steps involved in protein synthesis.

ribosome A complex of protein and RNA that catalyzes the synthesis of proteins.

rough endoplasmic reticulum (rough ER) Endoplasmic reticulum that has ribosomes bound to its outer surface.

Saccharomyces Genus of budding yeast that are frequently used in the study of eukaryote cell biology.

sarcoma Cancer of connective tissue.

Schwann cell Glia cell that produces myelin in the peripheral nervous system.

screening Checking for disease when there are no symptoms.

senescence Physical and biochemical changes that occur in cells and organisms with age.

signal transduction A process by which a signal is relayed to the interior of a cell where it elicits a response at the cytoplasmic or nuclear level.

smooth muscle cell Muscles lining the intestinal tract and arteries. Lacks the striations typical of cardiac and skeletal muscle, giving it a smooth appearance when viewed under a microscope.

somatic cell Any cell in a plant or animal except those that produce gametes (germ cells or germ cell precursors).

somatic cell nuclear transfer Animal cloning technique whereby a somatic cell nucleus is transferred to an enucleated oocyte. Synonomous with cell nuclear replacement.

Southern blotting The transfer of DNA fragments from an agarose gel to a piece of nylon filter paper. Specific fragments are identified by hybridizing the filter to a labeled probe. Invented by the Scottish scientist E. M. Southern in 1975.

stem cell Pluripotent progenitor cell, found in embryos and various parts of the body, that can differentiate into a wide variety of cell types.

steroid A hydrophobic molecule with a characteristic four-ringed structure. Sex hormones, such as estrogen and testosterone, are steroids.

structural gene A gene that codes for a protein or an RNA. Distinguished from regions of the DNA that are involved in regulating gene expression but are non-coding.

synapse A neural communication junction between an axon and a dendrite. Signal transmission occurs when neurotransmitters, released into the junction by the axon of one neuron, stimulate receptors on the dendrite of a second neuron.

syncytium A large multinucleated cell. Skeletal muscle cells are syncytiums produced by the fusion of many myoblasts.

syngeneic transplants A patient receives tissue or an organ from an identical twin.

tamoxifen A drug that is used to treat breast cancer. Tamoxifen blocks the effects of the hormone estrogen in the body. It belongs to the family of drugs called antiestrogens.

T cell (T lymphocyte) A white blood cell involved in activating and coordinating the immune response.

telomere The end of a chromosome. Replaced by the enzyme telomerase with each round of cell division to prevent shortening of the chromosomes.

telophase The final stage of mitosis in which the chromosomes decondense and the nuclear envelope reforms.

template A single strand of DNA or RNA whose sequence serves as a guide for the synthesis of a complementary, or daughter, strand.

therapeutic cloning The cloning of a human embryo for the purpose of harvesting the inner cell mass (ES cells).

topoisomerase An enzyme that makes reversible cuts in DNA to relieve strain or to undo knots.

transcription The copying of a DNA sequence into RNA, catalyzed by RNA polymerase.

transcriptional factor A general term referring to a wide assortment of proteins needed to initiate or regulate transcription.

transfection Introduction of a foreign gene into a eukaryote cell.

transfer RNA (tRNA) A collection of small RNA molecules that transfer an amino acid to a growing polypeptide chain on a ribosome. There is a separate tRNA for amino acid.

transgenic organism A plant or animal that has been transfected with a foreign gene.

trans-Golgi network   The membrane surfaces where glycoproteins and glycolipids exit the Golgi complex in transport vesicles.

translation   A ribosome-catalyzed process whereby the nucleotide sequence of an mRNA is used as a template to direct the synthesis of a protein.

transposable element (transposon)   A segment of DNA that can move from one region of a genome to another.

ultrasound (ultrasonography)   A procedure in which high-energy sound waves (ultrasound) are bounced off internal tissues or organs producing echoes that are used to form a picture of body tissues (a sonogram).

umbilical cord blood stem cells   Stem cells, produced by a human fetus and the placenta, that are found in the blood that passes from the placenta to the fetus.

vector   A virus or plasmid used to carry a DNA fragment into a bacterial cell (for cloning) or into a eukaryote to produce a transgenic organism.

vesicle   A membrane-bounded bubble found in eukaryote cells. Vesicles carry material from the ER to the Golgi and from the Golgi to the cell membrane.

virus   A particle containing an RNA or DNA genome surrounded by a protein coat. Viruses are cellular parasites that cause many diseases.

western blotting   The transfer of protein from a polyacrylamide gel to a piece of nylon filter paper. Specific proteins are detected with labeled antibodies. The name was inspired by the original blotting technique invented by E. M. Southern.

yeast   Common term for unicellular eukaryotes that are used to brew beer and make bread. Bakers yeast, *Saccharomyces cerevisiae,* is also widely used in studies on cell biology.

zygote   A diploid cell produced by the fusion of a sperm and egg.

FURTHER READING

Alberts, Bruce. *Essential Cell Biology.* New York: Garland Publishing, 1998. Albumin.org. "Human Serum Albumin." Available online. URL: http://www.albumin.org. Accessed on October 12, 2003.

The Associated Press. "Cloned Cows Die in California." April 3, 2001. Available online. URL: http://news.excite.com/news/ap/010403/00/cloned-cows. Accessed on October 12, 2003.

Dynamic Development. University of Calgary, Alberta, Canada. "Historical Roots of Developmental Biology." Available online. URL: http://www.ucalgary.ca/~browder/roots.html. Accessed on February 20, 2004.

———. "Mammalian Cloning." Available online. URL: http://www.ucalgary.ca/UofC/eduweb/virtualembryo/cloning.html. Accessed on March 9, 2004.

Genetic Science Learning Center. University of Utah, U.S.A. "Human Genetics." Available online. URL: http://gslc.genetics.utah.edu. Accessed on February 20, 2004.

Holstein Canada. "The Holstein Breed." Available online. URL: http://www.holstein.ca/English/Breed/index.asp. Accessed on March 9, 2004.

Institute of Molecular Biotechnology. Jena, Germany. "Molecules of Life." Available online. URL: http://www.imb-jena.de/IMAGE.html. Accessed on February 20, 2004.

Kolata, Gina. Clone: *The Road to Dolly and the Path Ahead.* New York: William Morrow, 1998.

Krstic, R. V. *Illustrated Encyclopedia of Human Histology.* New York: Springer-Verlag, 1984.

Lentz, Thomas L. *Cell Fine Structure: An Atlas of Drawings of Whole-Cell Structure.* Philadelphia: Saunders, 1971.

Mader, Sylvia S. *Inquiry into Life.* Boston: McGraw-Hill, 2003.

Nature. "Double Helix: 50 Years of DNA." Many articles assembled by the journal to commemorate the 50th anniversary of James Watson and Francis Crick's classic paper describing the structure of DNA. Available online. URL: http://www.nature.com/nature/dna50/index.html. Accessed on October 12, 2003.

Nature Science Update. "Dolly Makes Museum Debut." April 11, 2003. Available online. URL: http://www.nature.com/nsu/030407/030407-11.html. Accessed on October 12, 2003.

The New York Times. "President Bush Presses for Ban on Human Cloning." April 10, 2002. Available online. URL: http://www.nytimes.com/aponline/national/AP-Bush.html. Accessed on October 12, 2003.

———. "Mule in Idaho Is First Member of Horse Family to Be Cloned." May 29, 2003. Available online. URL: http://www.nytimes.com/2003/05/29/science/29WIRE-MULE.html. Accessed on October 12, 2003.

Roslin Institute. "Potential Benefits of Cloning and Nuclear Transfer." Available online. URL: http://www2.ri.bbsrc.ac.uk/library/research/cloning/nt-benefits2.html. Accessed on October 12, 2003.

Scientific Registry of Transplant Recipients. "Organ Transplants." Available online. URL: http://www.ustransplant.org/annual_reports/ar02/ar02_main_organ.htm. Accessed on October 12, 2003.

University of Louisville Health Sciences Center. "The Implantable Artificial Heart Project." Available online. URL: http://www.heartpioneers.com. Accessed on October 12, 2003.

University of Maryland Medicine. "Transplantation Statistics." Available online. URL: http://www.umm.edu/transplant/stats-all.html. Accessed on October 12, 2003.

Washington Post. "Debate About Cloning Returns to Congress." January 30, 2003. Available online. URL: http://www.washingtonpost.com/ac2/wp-dyn?pagename=article&node=&contentId=A63303-2003Jan29. Accessed on October 12, 2003.

Washington Post. "House Votes to Prohibit Human Cloning." February 28, 2003. Available online. URL: http://www.washingtonpost.com/ac2/wp-dyn/A13624-2003Feb27. Accessed on October 12, 2003.

———. "U.S. Seeks to Extend Ban on Cloning." February 27, 2002. Available online. URL: http://www.washingtonpost.com/ac2/

wp-dyn?pagename=article&node=&contentId=A8119-2002Feb26. Accessed on October 12, 2003.

Wells, H. G. *The Island of Doctor Moreau.* Available online. URL: http://www.online-literature.com/wellshg/doctormoreau.

The Whitehouse.gov. "Statement by the President." Human cloning policy statement issued by President Bush on February 27, 2003. Available online. URL: http://www.whitehouse.gov/news/releases/2003/02/print/20030227-20.html. Accessed on October 12, 2003.

Wilmut, Ian, Keith Campbell and Colin Tudge. *The Second Creation.* New York: Farrar, Straus & Giroux, 2000.

WEB SITES

The Department of Energy Human Genome Project (United States). Covers every aspect of the human genome project with extensive color illustrations. http://www.ornl.gov/TechResources/Human_Genome/. Accessed on October 12, 2003.

Genetic Science Learning Center at the Eccles Institute of Human Genetics, University of Utah. An excellent resource for beginning students. This site contains information and illustrations covering basic cell biology, animal cloning, gene therapy, and stem cells. http://gslc.genetics.utah.edu. Accessed on October 12, 2003.

Institute of Molecular Biotechnology, Jena/Germany. Image Library of Biological Macromolecules. http://www.imb-jena.de/IMAGE.html. Accessed on October 12, 2003.

National Center for Biotechnology Information (NCBI). This site, established by the National Institutes of Health, is an excellent resource for anyone interested in biology. The NCBI provides access to GenBank (DNA sequences), literature databases (Medline and others), molecular databases, and topics dealing with genomic biology. With the literature database, for example, anyone can access Medline's 11 million biomedical journal citations to research biomedical questions. Many of these links provide free access to full-length research papers. http://www.ncbi.nlm.nih.gov. Accessed on October 12, 2003.

The National Human Genome Research Institute (United States). The institute supports genetic and genomic research, including the

ethical, legal, and social implications of genetics research. http://
www.genome.gov/. Accessed on October 12, 2003.

National Institutes of Health (NIH, United States). The NIH posts
information on their Web site that covers a broad range of topics,
including general health information, cell biology, aging, cancer
research, and much more. http://www.nih.gov. Accessed on October 12, 2003.

Nature. The journal *Nature* has provided a comprehensive guide to the
human genome. This site provides links to the definitive historical
record for the sequences and analyses of human chromosomes. All
papers can be downloaded for free and are based on the final draft
produced by the Human Genome Project. http://www.nature.com/
nature/focus/humangenome/. Accessed on October 12, 2003.

Organ Transplantation links. http://www.ishlt.org/links/transplant
RelatedOrganizations.asp. Accessed on October 12, 2003.

Roslin Institute. The place where Dolly was sheep was cloned. Provides
illustrated articles about the cloning of Dolly and other animals.
http://www.roslin.ac.uk. Accessed on October 12, 2003.

The Sanger Institute (United Kingdom). DNA-sequencing center
named after Fred Sanger, inventor of the most commonly used
method for sequencing DNA. The institute is also involved in projects that apply human DNA sequence data to find cures for cancer
and other medical disorders. http://www.sanger.ac.uk. Accessed on
October 9, 2003.

United Network for Organ Sharing. http://www.unos.org/data/about/
viewDataReports.asp. Accessed on October 12, 2003.

The United States Food and Drug Administration. Provides extensive
coverage of general health issues and regulations. http://www.fda.
gov. Accessed on October 12, 2003.

The White House. Provides links to policy statements and presidential
directives concerning human cloning. http://www.whitehouse.gov.
Accessed on October 12, 2003.

INDEX

❊